Medical difficulties

IDENTIFYING AND SUPPORTING NEEDS • ACTIVITIES COVERING EARLY LEARNING GOALS • WORKING WITH PARENTS

DR HANNAH MORTIMER

Author
Dr Hannah Mortimer

Editor
Sally Gray

Assistant Editor
Saveria Mezzana

Series Designers
Sarah Rock/Anna Oliwa

Designer
Anna Oliwa

Illustrations
Debbie Clark

Cover artwork
Claire Henley

Acknowledgements
Qualifications and Curriculum Authority for the use of extracts from the
QCA/DfEE document *Curriculum guidance for the foundation stage*
© 2000, Qualifications and Curriculum Authority.

The author wishes to thank the Children's Centre in Northallerton for general information
and advice, and Helen Robinson for thinking of the tear bottle.
Every effort has been made to trace copyright holders and the publishers apologize for any
inadvertent omissions.

Text © 2002, Hannah Mortimer
© 2002, Scholastic Ltd

Designed using Adobe Pagemaker

Published by Scholastic Ltd, Villiers House,
Clarendon Avenue, Leamington Spa, Warwickshire CV32 5PR

Visit our website at www.scholastic.co.uk

Printed by Alden Group Ltd, Oxford

1 2 3 4 5 6 7 8 9 0   2 3 4 5 6 7 8 9 0 1

British Library Cataloguing-in-Publication Data A catalogue record for this book is
available from the British Library.

ISBN 0 439 01991 5

Medical difficulties

CONTENTS · CONTENTS · CONTENTS · CONTENTS · CONTENTS

KNOWLEDGE AND UNDERSTANDING OF THE WORLD

PHYSICAL DEVELOPMENT

CREATIVE DEVELOPMENT

PHOTOCOPIABLES

INTRODUCTION

All children feel unwell from time to time, and some may have more serious or long-term illnesses or medical conditions. In this book, there are ideas for including these children in your daily activities and your planning.

The aims of the series

There are now clear recommendations from the DfES about planning for children's medical conditions. There is also a revised *Code of Practice* for the identification and assessment of special educational needs (SEN), and settings will require guidance on what these changes mean to them. Early years educators are sometimes confused about medical difficulties and the overlap with 'special needs'. This book will make the legal framework clearer for them.

In addition, the QCA Early Learning Goals emphasize the key role that early years educators play in identifying needs and responding quickly to them. While most educators feel that an inclusive approach is the best one for all the children concerned, they often need guidance on what an inclusive early years curriculum might actually 'look like' in practice.

Within this series, there are books on helping children with most kinds of special or medical needs:
- behavioural and emotional difficulties
- speech and language difficulties
- learning difficulties
- physical and co-ordination difficulties
- autistic spectrum difficulties
- medical difficulties
- sensory difficulties.

An eighth book forms a handbook for the whole series: *Special Needs Handbook*. It provides general guidance and more detail on how to assess, plan for, teach and monitor those children who have special educational needs in early years settings.

Most groups will, at some point, include children who have medical difficulties or conditions. This book will help all early years professionals to understand such difficulties and to provide inclusive activities. It will also help them to keep in touch with children who are ill at home or in hospital.

Who this book is for

This book will be helpful for those working in early years settings. It provides practical ideas and information for teachers in nursery and Reception classes and for those who work in pre-schools, private nurseries and day nurseries. It is also

helpful to nursery nurses who support children in hospitals, hospices and day wards, and for teachers who work in paediatric wards. The activities will also provide ideas for parents, carers and childminders nursing a sick child at home.

How to use this book

The format of this book is slightly different from the others in the series since children who have medical difficulties do not necessarily have special educational needs, and it would not be appropriate to suggest 'special' approaches for them.

In Chapter 1, you will find an introduction to the legal requirements towards children who have medical difficulties. You will be reminded of the requirements of the QCA Early Learning Goals and Curriculum Guidelines across each Area of Learning. You will be helped to develop policies and procedures for your setting, and introduced to the need for individual health care plans. The overlap with special educational needs will be discussed and there will be information about how you can best liaise with parents and carers and with Health Service professionals.

In Chapter 2, the needs of children who have medical difficulties are looked at in more detail. You will find information on the kinds of conditions and needs that are covered in the book. The question of how young children view illness is raised, and consideration is given to what the educational implications are for them and your setting. There is also information regarding approaches such as relaxation and distraction for the control of discomfort and pain. Ways of keeping the absent child in touch with your setting are also discussed.

In Chapter 3, there follows information about the medical conditions themselves, providing details about their prevalence and causes. Information will be given about some medical conditions that you might come across, including eczema, asthma, diabetes, epilepsy, HIV and AIDS, cancer, meningitis and cystic fibrosis. Consideration is given to the implications of these conditions for the early years practitioner and advice is given on how to help and support children and families who are affected.

Six activity chapters follow, each related to one of the QCA Areas of Learning: Personal, social and emotional development; Communication, language and literacy; Mathematical development; Knowledge and understanding of the world; Physical development and Creative development. Each chapter contains eight activities, each with a learning objective for all the children (with or without medical needs)

and an individual learning target for any child who might have any one of a range of medical difficulties. The activities target different kinds of difficulties in the hope that early years workers will become able to develop a flexible approach to planning inclusive activities, dipping into the ideas that pepper these chapters. It is suggested that you read through them all for their general ideas, and then select activities as and when you need them as part of your general curriculum planning.

Each activity also provides information about the size of group for which the activity might be appropriate, a list of what you need, a description of what to do, any special support which might be necessary for the child with medical difficulties, ideas for extending the activity for more able children, and suggestions for links with home. It is recommended that you use these guidelines flexibly and be guided by the needs of the children in your particular setting.

Though this book relates to the early years and medical procedures followed in England, the general guidance will be equally relevant to early years practitioners in Wales, Scotland and Northern Ireland as the ideas apply equally well to the documents for pre-school education in these countries.

Children's health

Nowadays, children are much healthier than they used to be thanks to better living conditions, better nutrition and more effective treatments. Nevertheless, children do suffer from frequent infections and are likely to be feeling 'under the weather' from time to time. Viral infections such as colds and influenza do not respond to antibiotics, and children need time and convalescence in order to allow their natural body defences to fight the infections. When a child is feeling unwell, they tend to become quieter and to withdraw into themselves. You will find yourself offering different approaches to an unmotivated child, providing more comfort and support and carrying out activities that are gentle, motivating and distracting for the child. Many of the activities in this book will be just as helpful for children with short-term medical discomfort as for those with chronic medical conditions.

Medical conditions

Approximately 10 to 15 per cent of children under sixteen are affected by chronic, long-term physical problems. The most common conditions are eczema (8 to 10 per cent of children), asthma (2 to 5 per cent), diabetes (1.8 per cent), congenital heart disease (0.2 to 0.7 per cent) and epilepsy (0.26 to 0.46 per cent). There are many other potentially frightening and/or painful conditions which are less common, and many of these have an unpredictable course. They include sickle-cell anaemia, rheumatoid arthritis, HIV infections and AIDS, cystic fibrosis, cancer and leukaemia.

There are also life-threatening conditions which are very rare and extremely stressful for the child and family, such as kidney disease, metabolic disorders (where the body's chemistry is affected) and neuromuscular conditions (such as muscular dystrophy). You will find more information about some of the conditions that affect movement and balance in the book *Physical and Co-ordination Difficulties* by Dr Hannah Mortimer in this series.

Using a wide variety of resources

The activities in this book make use of a wide range of materials and resources. Most children's wards in hospitals now carry plenty of toys and games for learning. Settings might find it helpful to build up a special box of resources for lending to a child who is away for a period of time due to illness. You will find that most of the activities suitable for home involve materials which can be used in bed or when the child is resting and recovering.

Links with home

Sometimes children with illness or medical conditions need prolonged periods at home for treatment or recovery. If links can be kept going between your setting and the home, the child and family will continue to feel involved in what you are doing and the child will find it easier to return to you once they are feeling better or once their treatment is finished. Be guided by the parents or carers who will know how ready their child is to become more active and involved again. These days, children are encouraged to engage in play as soon as possible following major illness or surgery, so that they can become alert and interested again in their surroundings. Gentle distraction is a wonderful way to take a child's mind off their discomfort or fears.

Providing special support for families

A major illness in a child or a new medical diagnosis can be devastating for a family. It might be that they are in greatest need of support and friendship at the point when they are confined to hospital with their child. Your cards and best wishes will help them feel that you are thinking about them and caring, even when their child is not with you. Look for ways of providing a listening ear to support.

Sometimes, you may be involved in supporting a family whose child has died. Consider keeping the links with the family going so that friendships and lines of support can be continued and so that you can share photographs and happy memories – it is through sharing the happy memories that their child's memory lives on.

THE LEGAL REQUIREMENTS

Children with long-term medical conditions may require special approaches and planning. In this chapter you will learn how to write individual health care plans for the children who need them and how to work alongside other professionals.

The legal framework for children with medical needs

Most children will, at some point, have a medical condition that may affect their ability to join in with your activities. For many of them, this will be short-term – perhaps they are simply finishing off a course of medication. These children do not have SEN and they are not disabled in any way. Other pupils have longer-term medical conditions that

could limit their access to education if not properly managed. These children are described as having 'medical needs'. These are the children for whom you should draw up an 'individual health care plan' (see page 13).

If you are working with a child who has a common medical condition such as eczema or asthma, you will be providing just the same early years curriculum as for any other child within your setting. You will also be following your usual health and safety guidelines for children and staff. There are no additional and 'special' legal frameworks that you should work under. You could not say that these children had 'special educational needs' unless they were so badly affected by their condition

that it prevented their early learning and educational progress. Neither would it make sense to say that they were 'disabled' in any way. In this book, you will find more information about common medical conditions in Chapter 3, and many activities will help to distract the children when they are feeling uncomfortable.

However, if you are working with children who have chronic, long-term and significant medical conditions, then these children might fall under the legal framework for supporting children with disabilities or with special educational needs. The definitions of disabled children and children with SEN are different. A child might be disabled *and* have SEN, or a child might be one without the other.

The Children's Act 1989 says that a child is disabled if they are blind, deaf or dumb, or suffers from a mental disorder. They might also be disabled if they have been permanently and seriously handicapped by an illness, injury or a birth deformity. The Disability Discrimination Act 1995 says that people are disabled if they have a physical or mental impairment that has a substantial and long-term adverse effect on their ability to carry out normal day-to-day activities. It is clear that this definition is wide and will include many children who also have special educational needs.

Which children also have SEN?

A child has SEN if they have a learning difficulty that calls for 'special educational provision' to be made for them. In other words, a child has SEN if you find that you need to adapt and differentiate your activities to take account of their individual needs. In turn, a child has a learning difficulty if they have a significantly greater difficulty in learning than others the same age. A child also has a learning difficulty if there is a disability that prevents or hinders them from making use of educational facilities (of a kind generally provided for children of the same age in schools within the local education authority).

For more information about the legal framework for meeting special educational needs, you may refer to the handbook for this series,

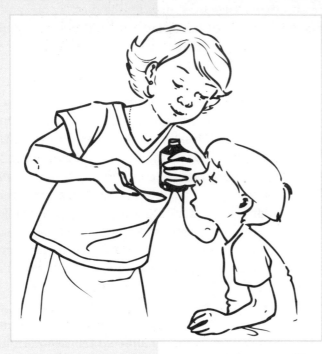

Special Needs Handbook by Dr Hannah Mortimer. The guidance can be found in the DfES's *SEN Code of Practice*, which has been updated to include the Disability Act 2001 and introduced to settings in 2002.

In this book, we will go on to look at the government guidelines for supporting children with medical needs. What suggestions are made for 'good practice' in your setting?

Developing policies and procedures for your setting

The DfEE and the Department of Health have published a pack entitled *Supporting Pupils with Medical Needs*, which helps you to draw up a policy for working with these children. If you can show that you respond positively to children who have medical needs, you will be encouraging a positive attitude from all your colleagues and children. It is strongly recommended that you develop your own policies for managing medication and supporting medical conditions, depending on your local situation. This chapter aims to help you do this.

Thinking about medication

One of the first things you might like to think about is how you feel about giving medication in your setting. The employer (usually the LEA, school governing body or management committee) is responsible for making sure that your setting has a health and safety policy, and this should include how you will support children with medical needs and how you will manage medication. Employers should also make sure that their insurance covers any staff involved in medication. If there is ever a complication following medication, accurate policies, agreements and records will be essential.

Parents or carers and the Head of the setting should reach a joint agreement about the children's medication. You should respect any cultural or religious views that the children's carers hold. Ideally, the Head should seek the carers' agreement before passing on medical information to colleagues.

When making a policy, you will need to consider the following:
● whether the Head accepts responsibility for colleagues giving medication in the setting;
● if and when children can be given non-prescription medication such as paracetamol solution and sticking plasters;
● the need for carers' written agreement for any medication or treatment to be given in your setting, prescription or otherwise;
● staff training for medical matters;
● record-keeping;
● storage and access to medication;
● how your setting intends to support children with long-term medical needs;
● the setting's emergency procedures.

There is no legal duty that requires you to administer medication. However, it can be very helpful to the child and their family, and make all the difference between whether or not a child can attend your setting. If you are going to volunteer to administer medication, you need clear information and support from the particular child's carers. It is parents or guardians who have the prime responsibility for their child's health, and they should provide your setting with everything you need to know about their child's medical condition and needs. You might also find it helpful to contact the local school doctor, health visitor or nurse for general advice for managing medical conditions and medication.

If you are giving medication with parental agreement, you should still check the child's name, the written instructions, the prescribed dose and the expiry date on the container. A child under 12 should never be given aspirin unless it has been prescribed by a doctor.

Storing medication

You should not need to store large amounts of medicine – ask parents and carers to send in just the daily dose if possible. Each container should be clearly marked with the child's name, the dose and the instructions. Medicines should be locked away and staff should know where the key is kept. Some medicines need to be kept in the refrigerator. If this is a food refrigerator, keep medicines in a special sealed container within it. Your local pharmacy should be willing to provide you with information about storing different kinds of medicines.

Do not dispose of medicines yourself. Give unused medicines back to carers – they are responsible for the disposal and replacement of medicines.

Coping with emergencies

You will need to know what constitutes an emergency for a particular child's condition. Ensure that someone in your setting is designated as being responsible for carrying out emergency procedures. Make sure that you have an up-to-date emergency contact list for each child in the setting. If an ambulance is called, a member of staff should accompany the child and stay with them until the parents or carers arrive.

Generally, you should not take children to hospital in your own car, though there may be occasions when this decision has to be made. In this case, the member of staff should be accompanied by another colleague, and public liability vehicle insurance is needed.

Individual health care plans

The purpose of the individual health care plan is to identify what kind of medical support a child will need in your setting. It should be agreed with the parents or carers and reviewed every six months or so, or as a child's condition changes. Whether or not you decide to make a plan does not depend on a particular condition so much as how the condition affects the child. One child's eczema may not affect them much at all, while another child's might be extremely uncomfortable and distracting. An example of the plan is shown on page 13.

The photocopiable pro forma on page 85 provides an individual health care plan for you to use or adapt. Contributors to the plan might include the Head of the setting, parents or carers, class teacher and any care assistant, doctor or nurse who is involved. Staff directly involved with the child will need to understand the child's personal symptoms and how they should provide daily care. It is important that they know what constitutes an emergency for the child and what action should be taken in an emergency. There may be other information which staff do not need to know because it is confidential and it does not impinge on the child's life in the setting. The Head of the setting should agree what is confidential information and what will be shared, out of necessity, with colleagues.

Working with parents and carers

Parents and carers are responsible for making sure that their children are well enough to attend your setting and for passing on to you sufficient information to help you support their children's medical condition. Sharing information between setting and home is important if you are going to ensure the best care for the child. If carers themselves feel that they need more information and training about their children's medical condition, then you might like to put them in touch with your local School Health Service or one of the voluntary organizations on page 94.

Working with Health Service professionals

Sometimes the School Health Service will provide special training on certain medical conditions. You might be able to ask for general advice to help you support children with certain conditions. You might also find the local health visitor a useful contact. If you need to help the children use specialist equipment in your setting, there will usually be a specialist nurse or therapist who will be able to give you guidance. Parents and carers are also an excellent resource for showing you when to respond to a child's symptoms and what to do about them.

Health and hygiene

Use your common sense to ensure that your setting is hygienic and as germ-free as possible. Children should not share spoons or face-cloths. They should be encouraged to wash their hands when needed and before handling food. Encourage them to blow their noses and dispose of the tissues safely. Staff also need to use protective disposable gloves when dealing with spillages, blood or other bodily fluids. You will find more guidance in the DfES publication *HIV and AIDS: A Guide for the Education Service*.

Individual health care plan   CONFIDENTIAL

Name: Shannon   **Age:** 3

People contributing to this plan: Dr Raj (GP) by letter, Jen Schmidt (health visitor), Sheena (Shannon's Mum), Perveen (SENCO) and Tracey (key worker).

Date of plan: April 2002

Medical condition: Shannon has severe eczema on his limbs, his trunk and his head.

Child's personal symptoms: Shannon gets very uncomfortable when he is hot and sweaty, and can also become sore when he has been scratching and rubbing.

Daily care requirements:
● When Shannon begins to scratch or rub, keep him distracted with something to play using his hands.
● Try to keep the temperature of the room moderate. Encourage light and loose cotton clothing.
● Put gloves on when it is cold outside.
● When his eczema is very bad, Sheena will send in his special cream and tell us how often and where to apply this.
● When the eczema is very bad, Shannon may have to wear special dressings. Again, Sheena will tell us each morning if we need to do anything about these. They must be kept dry.
● We have a special solution from the doctor to add to the water tray to prevent skin drying out. Sheena will tell us if he is not to get his hands wet any day.
● Shannon cannot handle clay. He can manage play dough so long as he washes and dries his hands afterwards and applies some of his cream.
● Remember that Shannon might be very tired. Provide somewhere quiet for him to lie down if he has not slept well the night before.
● Sheena will use a home–setting diary to keep us in touch and we will fill it in daily as well to let her know how Shannon has been.

What constitutes an emergency for the child?
● There should be no real emergencies. Call Sheena if he gets very distressed with himself.

Any follow-up care:
The health visitor will call in to the setting to see how Shannon is managing, and offer any advice. It is expected that the severity of Shannon's condition will lessen as he gets older.

Emergency contacts:
1. Name: Sheena   **Relationship:** Mother
Phone nos: home: work:

2. Name: Pat   **Relationship:** Grandmother
Phone nos: home: work:

Clinic/hospital contact: Name: Jen Schmidt   **Phone no:**
GP: Name: Dr Raj, Appletree Practice   **Phone no:**

Next review date with parents: September 2002 (date to be arranged)

Some parents or carers of children who are medically frail might need you to tell them when certain infections are going around your setting. Be conscious of rubella infections if you have pregnant mothers assisting. Be wary of chicken pox and bad infections if you have a child who is HIV-positive.

Most carers of otherwise healthy children will be thankful for them to catch the usual childhood infections early and to develop immunity to them before school.

Requirements of the Early Learning Goals

Registered early years providers are expected to deliver a broad and balanced curriculum across the six Areas of Learning as defined in the Early Learning Goals and the *Curriculum Guidance for the Foundation Stage* (QCA). The introduction of the Early Learning Goals has paved

the way for children's early learning to be followed through into Baseline Assessment measures on entry to school (from September 1998) and into National Curriculum assessment for school-age children. It is expected that the integration of these procedures will contribute to the earlier identification of children who are experiencing difficulties in making progress.

Trouble has been taken to set the Early Learning Goals into context so that they are seen as an aid to planning ahead rather than as an early years curriculum to replace 'learning through play'. Effective early years education needs both a relevant curriculum and practitioners who understand it and are able to implement it. To this end, practical examples of Stepping Stones towards the Early Learning Goals are provided in the detailed curriculum guidance.

Within this book, each activity (from Chapter 4 to Chapter 9) is linked to a learning objective for all the children in the group, and also to an individual learning target for any child who has medical difficulties.

Defining a set of learning goals which most children will have attained by the end of their Foundation Stage (the end of their Reception year) has helped to ensure that nursery education is of good quality and a sound preparation for later schooling. Early years providers registered with their local Early Years Development and Childcare Partnership are required to have their educational provision inspected regularly. The nursery inspectors, appointed by the Office for Standards in Education (OFSTED) assess the quality of the early years educational provision and look at the clarity of roles and responsibilities within the setting. They are also interested in plans for meeting the needs of individual children (including those with special educational needs) and in how the setting intends to develop improved partnership with parents and carers.

HELPING CHILDREN WITH MEDICAL DIFFICULTIES

This chapter examines how very young children think about illness and explains what you can do to support them and help their understanding. It also provides ideas for keeping in touch with absent children.

Learning about illness

If children are born with a chronic medical condition, this is bound to affect the way they see themselves and their world. They may not realize that there is something 'different' about themselves until they start in your group and meet other children. Perhaps they gradually begin to notice that not every child has to have daily injections or to use inhalers. In this situation, the child does not suddenly see themselves as having a medical condition – rather, it is a gradual realization as they become old enough to compare themselves with others.

Once they begin to understand that they are ill, the child will still not know much about their specific condition – they will know more about what it means *to them*. They will gradually add to this knowledge and modify it as they grow older and understand more. Some children actively seek out this information and are keen to know more. Others will find this difficult and tend to 'opt out' of learning more. Others still will find it hard to accept that they might not get better; after all, their parents or carers have always 'fixed' everything for them before.

Relating information

Children will gradually come to understand more about their condition from accurate sources as well as from television and gossip. Parents and carers will need to keep this information factual and correct, relating it in practical terms to what it means for their children at a level that they can understand.

How do children learn to make sense of what is happening to their bodies? Most of a very young child's knowledge comes from what is actually happening to them. They can only think in concrete terms about the events that are happening and the 'here and now'. They cannot begin to think about the long-term future and to reflect on 'what if I *wasn't* ill?'.

How bodies work

Very young children are usually interested in their own bodies and this makes a useful topic for your group. At first, they will delight in looking at and naming different parts of their bodies. They will enjoy action rhymes and songs associated with moving different body parts.

Once they begin to understand the concept of 'inside', they can begin to understand what is happening *inside* their bodies too. At first, their understanding of this might be very immature. The skin might be seen simply as a container or bag for all the bones and blood inside. This is why some children can become very frightened of minor wounds or injections because they fear that their insides might fall out. For this reason, plasters are reassuring (but check with parents and carers that they are not allergic to the adhesive first). A simple explanation about healing and skin growing back can help to reassure the children.

Five-year-olds will be developing a simple understanding of the main organs within the body and will usually be aware that they have a heart, a brain and a tummy. They tend to give them simple explanations based on what they actually see or feel: 'my tummy is for rumbling' and 'my lungs are for going in and out'.

Children with a particular condition, such as a heart condition, will come to understand more about this organ at an early age but will still not understand how their whole body might be affected by their condition.

A child's view of illness

How do young children think about illness? Very young children will typically fret and turn to the parent and carer to 'kiss it better' or 'fix it' in some way. They will not necessarily understand that a doctor or nurse can help this process, and may be distressed during medical treatments. That is why it is so important for a familiar person to stay close to and comfort a young child in hospital or clinic. Children of three to five years can understand that they hurt or that something is wrong with them, but do not always have the words to explain this. It is usually left to the familiar adult to interpret what they are trying to say. For example, a three-year-old with a tummy ache might say, 'I got a headache in my tummy'. They also tend to see illness as something which is broken and say, for example, 'My heart is broken'. In the same way, they might see medical treatments as 'fixing' the broken body and find it hard to understand why it does not always 'get better'. As children get older, parents and carers need to find the words to explain what is

happening as honestly as possible. They are supported in doing this by doctors, psychologists and specialist nurses.

Young children also develop ideas that certain treatments are 'magic', perhaps because we find this a helpful way to explain procedures and make them less frightening. Children talk of 'magic cream' which stops the injections hurting, and the 'magic machine' which makes their blood work. We need to be a little bit careful about not over-using this word. If we talk of a 'magic operation' to make a child better and it does not, then the child is left feeling frustrated and depressed. If we talk of death as a 'magic sleep', this can frighten children from going to sleep at night.

Sometimes young children see illness as a punishment for something they have done wrong. Again, we tend to reinforce this when we say things like, 'If you don't put your coat on, you'll catch pneumonia and have to go into hospital'. Children are more likely to think of illness as magic or a punishment if they do not have other explanations – so it is important to work with other professionals and carers to explain simply what is happening.

Four-year-olds are beginning to use questions and actions to explore and to solve problems. These children often see illness as being 'caught' in some way. In other words, they see all conditions and illnesses as relating to 'germs'. Sometimes this is a helpful explanation, but sometimes it misleads the child. For example, they cannot 'catch' diabetes or epilepsy from others; neither can they pass it on. As children grow older, they see that disabilities can be acquired through many different routes and that illness is an interplay of many different factors.

What you can do

When talking about a child's medical condition, concentrate on the 'here and now'. Help the child to find words for how they are feeling, what is happening and what will happen next.

Impending visits to hospital and clinics can be frightening until a child understands exactly what will happen. Talk with the parents or carers and carry out your regular play activities to help. Use imaginative play to introduce any potentially frightening experiences in a safe and

relaxed situation for the child. You will find plenty of ideas for doing this in the activity chapters of this book.

If you are carrying out a medical procedure such as giving an inhaler or changing a catheter, talk simply about what it is you are doing. Even if a child cannot understand everything you say, your calmness and tone of voice will be reassuring to them. The way that a child feels about their treatment is affected not only by their personal experiences, but also by how they are feeling at the time. If they are anxious and upset, this can make everything worse. They can quickly pick up anxiety from a parent or carer, so it is important that adults are prepared ahead for treatments and the possible reactions of the child.

Regular routines

Young children make sense of their world by mastering the familiar routines and rules that form their day. You can help in your setting by keeping routines as familiar as possible when a child has a chronic condition or illness. You can also make links between home and setting, or with hospital or hospice, so that you keep familiar activities and contacts going during a period of absence.

A day is a long time in the life of a child; three weeks is an eternity. It would be easy for a child to 'lose touch' with your group if you let contact drop, making the return to your setting all the more unsettling. It is a good idea to talk with the parents or carers well ahead of any planned absence, and offer contact in any unplanned absence of over a fortnight or so. You will find that many of the activities in this book provide ideas for keeping in touch with an absent child.

If a child has a particular appearance or needs particular equipment or medication in connection with their condition, then it might be that they only become self-conscious of this when they start in a new pre-school or school. Parents and carers can prepare them for this by talking through their condition with them and providing them with ideas for

how to answer other children's curious questions. The booklet *Starting Out* (see page 96) is a useful guide in this respect.

In the next chapter, you will read about the steps that you can take to support children with particular medical conditions. The more you understand about a particular condition, the calmer you will feel in dealing with any symptoms, and the easier it will be to apply your own common sense and early years knowledge.

By combining your experience of children's early learning with the information that you have read about a child's particular condition, you will be able to plan approaches that are tailor-made to the child's condition and level of understanding. The six activity chapters that follow Chapter 3 provide you with plenty of ideas. Since each child is unique, you will need to dip in and adapt the activities flexibly to suit your particular situation.

Thinking about siblings

The brothers and sisters of a child who is chronically ill or has a long-term medical condition may find it difficult to cope with the situation. They might resent the amount of attention that their sibling is receiving, though they might also feel guilty for doing so. Sometimes (and quite understandably), a young child might wish that his sister was not there. If the sister later goes into hospital or dies, the child is left feeling that this was his fault. Siblings, too, need clear explanations of what is happening, at a level that they can understand. Will they 'catch' the illness too? If they caught it from their brother (like catching a ball), would it save their brother from being ill? In your setting, you can give special attention and support to a child whose sibling is very ill, balancing the amount of attention and support they might need at this time. Again, you will find imaginary play a useful way of playing through situations and feelings.

With some treatments, brothers and sisters might not be able to visit hospital and could quickly feel out of touch with their sibling. They might feel anxious about what is happening, or act as if they have forgotten their sibling altogether. If a relative is ill at home, some young

children become distressed about coming to the setting because they are frightened that something dreadful might happen if they are not at home too. You might be able to support them in making pictures and creations for the carers to take into hospital, or for a sick relative at home.

Looking for special opportunities

Children who are frequently absent are bound to miss learning opportunities in your setting. It is particularly important to keep records of the activities the child has enjoyed so that you can identify 'gaps' in the early years curriculum and make up for missed opportunities. There might be some Areas of Learning that have to be left to one side for a while, such as Physical development. Nevertheless, with imagination and foresight, you will usually be able to find other ways of involving the child within their limitations.

Many of the ideas in Chapters 4 to 9 suggest activities which can be carried out from a bed, a children's ward or from home, and can be used by nursery nurses, parents or carers to keep the child included in the early years curriculum.

Most hospital wards now have play and craft areas with nursery nurses who will help to occupy children and involve them in play. Some of the activities in this book suggest ways of taking resources from your setting to hospital or home in order to provide activities for sick children. Other activities are specially adapted to suit a much narrower world or a child's bed rather than your large setting. In these activities, the materials used are kept small, and the focus of interest confined to the child's immediate surroundings.

There will be times when children are too ill or too preoccupied to learn actively. It is hard for a child to look and listen to what is going on around them if all they can attend to are the feelings inside them. There will, however, be times when they can be gently distracted and helped, through play, to relax and feel more comfortable.

Many of the activities in this book aim to provide enjoyment to the child and are intended to keep them feeling motivated. It is important to remember to stop when the child is feeling tired and to keep the activities gentle, short and successful. With a very poorly child, your aim will not be an *end-product* (such as teaching a child to read the letter 'b') so much as a *process* (keeping the child happy and occupied for fifteen minutes).

Staying in touch

Look for ways of keeping in touch with an absent child if they are away from you for more than a fortnight. This is a very long time to a young child, and friendships and familiarity can soon be lost. When a child recovers, it can be difficult not only to cope with leaving his parents or carers, but also to settle back into the setting. Many of the activities in this book provide you with ideas for doing this, not just helping the child who is ill, but also encouraging the other children in the setting to continue to include that child in their thoughts and activities.

Sometimes the children themselves will be able to think of ways in which they can keep in touch with an absent friend – for example, by making a special picture or card, a box of 'treasures' or a group letter. You might like to make a video or tape-recording of some of your songs and activities to send home, or to take some special photographs. Make use of the time when a child is not with you to help all the children understand what it means to be feeling very poorly and how hospitals, doctors and nurses can help. You will find references to some useful books for sharing with children about illness on page 95.

Trying a range of approaches

There are some approaches which have proved helpful when working with children who are chronically ill, and some ideas from these have been included in the activities.

● Imaginative play can be used to help children work through any anxieties or strong feelings that they have about worrying situations. Provide a hospital or clinic corner with a range of resources for encouraging the children to role-play together. Listening in will help you to see how a child is feeling and what level their understanding has reached.

● Art and craft time also provides good opportunities for encouraging children to express themselves and work through strong feelings.

● Puppet play and story time can also provide opportunities for talking together about illness and medical conditions.

There are references to books which introduce various medical conditions to children on page 95. Use some of these as part of your regular story time and then encourage talking and questioning afterwards, depending on the particular situation you are faced with.

If a child has recently been diagnosed with a serious or life-threatening condition, talk with the carers first about how and when they would like you to introduce the topic to the other children. Otherwise, introduce topics such as asthma and diabetes as part of your regular stories, so that these become familiar to the children.

● Relaxation techniques are valuable for helping children cope with pain and discomfort, and this is why many of the individual learning targets in the activities refer to enjoyment or include relaxation. It can be difficult to help very young children relax, and the easiest way is to keep your own voice and attitude calm, relaxing and reassuring. Slow breathing helps children to control muscle tension and anxiety, so another useful approach is to teach older children how to breathe slowly with you. A typical slow breath would be for you to breathe in for a slow count of 7 and out for 11.

'Visualization' has also been used to help children relax. Children can be helped to clear their minds and to imagine a warm, relaxing and safe place to go to. They can picture this in their minds and retreat to it when they need to feel warm and relaxed. Jenny Mosley suggests some helpful scripts for using with young children at circle time in order to encourage relaxation (see page 96).

The use of music and song also has a relaxing and distracting effect on children. Preoccupied children can be drawn into music time or soothed with the music that you play to them. Have a quiet area in your setting for relaxing in, with some calm music to listen to, soft cushions and picture books. This will be helpful to retreat to when a child is feeling out of sorts, but can also be used by any child who feels the need to be quiet for a while.

When a child dies

Though child mortality rates have fallen dramatically over the past thirty years, some of us are still likely to face the death of a child or a child's sibling at some point in our careers.

Causes of death

The greatest cause of death in a pre-school child in this country is from bacterial meningitis and respiratory disease. For fatal accidents, those that occur on our roads are the most common. Forty thousand families worldwide experience the death of a child every single day.

When a child in one of the families attending your setting dies, you will have your own grief and distress to cope with too. Try not to let your embarrassment and fear of not knowing what to say get in the way of speaking to the family. It can be devastating for them if, as well as the traumatic loss of their child, all the usual sources of friendship and support withdraw.

How to react

Let your care and concern show, and express your sorrow about what has happened. You are unlikely to be able to say that you understand what they are going through unless you have actually experienced such a loss yourself. Even then, everyone reacts to grief in their own individual way and at their own pace. Be aware that your own recent experience of any bereavement is going to become sharper as memories are revived.

Avoid giving direct advice and platitudes such as 'Time will heal' or 'You're taking it too well', but be sensitive to what practical help you can give. Perhaps you can provide additional support to any siblings or friends in your setting who are grieving in their own and individual ways. Never be frightened to mention the child's name – you will not add to the grief that is already so poignant, but it will provide opportunities for recognizing the child as a continuing part of your memories.

Find time to listen

Be there to listen. Allow the family's grief to show and be ready to talk about the child that they have lost. Find happy memories to share, and continue to talk about the child even after those first raw days. If you have lost a child in your nursery or class, find ways of at least offering the chance for regular contact with the family well into the future. You might think of a particularly appropriate and practical memorial within the group – a rocking horse, a special chair or a toy tractor.

Give extra attention

Do give extra attention to brothers and sisters who will be feeling confused and sad just when their parents or carers may not have the time or emotional resources to comfort them. Again, do not be afraid to talk about what has happened in clear, concrete terms, and play alongside the child, providing opportunities for them to act out some of their feelings. One nursery helped a brother and sister to draw pictures for their baby brother to say 'Goodbye', and these were taken to the hospital to be placed beside him.

The children in your group

The other children in your group will also want to talk about things and ask questions. Do not be put off if they seem almost callous in their response to a friend's death. The news is usually taken at a very practical level with concerns such as, 'Who will his mum collect from playgroup now?' or 'Who will get her bicycle?'. You may find some of the picture books mentioned on page 95 useful in introducing the topic of death in a way that makes sense for the young child.

Try to avoid using expressions which will confuse your children. If you talk of death being 'like going to sleep for ever', you can leave your children very frightened about what will happen if they allow themselves to fall asleep at night. Remember that the siblings may be feeling quite frightened that they too will die, and you may need to seek advice from the health visitor or specialist nurse on how to present the medical facts to the bereaved siblings.

Supporting the family

Do encourage the family to take things steadily and not try to do too much at once. They may need continual reassurance that what they did was right and the best for their child. Siblings may need reassurance too, so that they do not feel they caused or could have prevented the death in some way.

Never suggest to the parents that their other children will bring comfort – they can never replace the child that is lost. Above all, continue to listen and support the family; it will be a tremendous comfort that all the happy relationships formed when the child was with you can still go on. No one can erase the memories that continue.

MEDICAL CONDITIONS

This chapter provides descriptions of some of the many medical conditions and illnesses that might affect young children, and explains what you can do to help and support those in your setting who are affected by them.

The conditions covered

This chapter considers some of the most common medical conditions that you may encounter in your setting. Consideration is first given to conditions that affect many children, such as hay fever, eczema, asthma and allergies. Then more long-term conditions such as diabetes and epilepsy are discussed. Finally, there is information about some rarer conditions and infections such as HIV and AIDS, cancer and leukaemia, meningitis and cystic fibrosis.

With each condition or infection, we will look at the prevalence and causes, what it might mean for you in your setting, and what you can do to help. You will find more information about some of the conditions which affect movement and balance in *Physical and Co-ordination Difficulties* by Dr Hannah Mortimer in this series.

Hay fever
What is hay fever?

Some people react to certain substances by producing runny eyes and nose, itchiness or sneezing. They are reacting to the millions of tiny grains of pollen and spores that are found in the air, from trees, grasses, weeds, fungi and many other plants. These tiny grains irritate the membranes of the eyes and nose, causing an 'allergic rhinitis'.

Hay fever is one form of immediate allergic reaction triggered when our immune system becomes hypersensitive to certain things in the environment. Some children with hay fever are also allergic to other things and may have asthma or eczema too.

About one in seven people suffer from hay fever. This figure seems to be increasing. Some studies have blamed the increase of pollution in the air.

Hay fever is not contagious, despite the runny noses and sneezing. Children are not born with hay fever (though the pre-disposition can be hereditary). Instead, they can show the first signs of hay fever when they first come into contact with certain pollens – a child might actually develop the first signs of hay fever during their early years. Many hay-fever sufferers get better as they grow older.

What you can do

● Keep an eye on the environment outside your setting so that you can close windows if the traffic pollution is particularly bad or the pollen count high. (The pollen count will be given on local radio stations and in national newspapers.)

● Shut windows when grass is being mown outside and avoid playing outside for a while afterwards.

● Remember, families might not be aware that their child is developing hay fever yet, so be prepared with a pack of tissues and wipes during any outings to pollen-high areas.

● Be aware that some children with hay fever also feel lethargic and generally unwell when their symptoms are bad. Allow for quiet areas and activities for these children.

● If a child is very uncomfortable, stay calm and reassure them. Look for a quiet activity or story to distract them, and offer a clean damp flannel to soothe their eyes. Try to discourage them from rubbing their eyes and noses too much, and keep their hands clean.

● Talk with the parents or carers about what things seem to trigger their child's hay fever. You might need to avoid bringing in certain things for your nature table or displays (for example, bark, lichens and fresh flowers).

● Talk with the parents or carers about things that help, and make sure that they provide you with any sprays which the child might need.

● Some children with hay fever find sun-glasses to be a great help when playing outside – these can make sensitive eyes feel more comfortable in bright light.

● Take sensible precautions but aim to keep life as normal as possible for all the children.

Eczema

What is eczema?

Some children have a very itchy, dry, scaly, red rash on their faces, their necks, their hands and in the creases of their limbs. For some, this is widespread and can be debilitating; others just have patches. This is called 'eczema' and it is a very common allergic reaction. Members of families who suffer from hay fever and asthma also tend to have eczema. The most common form ('atopic eczema') typically develops in the first few months, and it disappears for most children by the time they are around three.

Eczema can be triggered by certain foods (such as dairy products, eggs or citrus fruit). An attack can also be set off by stress. Sometimes eczema is caused by skin irritants such as wool, washing detergents or pet fur.

What you can do

● Find out from the carers whether there are known triggers for their child's eczema. It may be that you need to make sure that the child avoids physical contact with pets or does not wear woolly clothes on their skin.
● Find out about any special diet. You may need to ask the carers to send in a special snack for their child or some soya milk instead of your usual supply.
● Ask whether there is anything that their child cannot play with. Some find playing with clay difficult as it can dry out the skin.
● Washing hands a lot can dry them out. Help the child to dry their hands thoroughly and ask the parents about a moisturizing (or 'emollient') cream if this will help.
● Consider adding a few drops of baby oil to your water tray if this would help a particular child. Wash the toys with warm soapy water at the end of the day to remove the film.
● Do not let your concern show itself as anxiety. If a child is irritated and upset by their condition, they need you to stay calm and to distract them as much as possible.
● Children with very severe eczema can get very tired if they had a particularly bad night. Provide a quiet area for rest and relaxation.
● Bear in mind that feather and down coverings and cushions can be a source of irritation for some children.

Asthma

What is asthma?

Children with asthma have a condition in which they cough, wheeze, have a tight chest and get short of breath. This is because their airways are almost always inflamed and sensitive. These airways react badly when the child has a cold or comes into contact with an asthma trigger. Common asthma triggers include colds, viral infections, pollen, cigarette smoke, house-dust mites, furry or feathery pets, exercise, air pollution, stress and even laughter.

Each child's asthma is different and each will react to different triggers. When the child's airways come into contact with a trigger, the lining starts to swell, mucus is secreted, and the muscles around the airways tighten. This makes the tubes in the lungs narrow and breathing becomes difficult. Children whose asthma has been identified will need to take a dose of reliever medication when this happens. This is usually given by inhaler. Some children need to use a preventer inhaler each day as well. Asthma symptoms can be very mild for some children, but extremely severe for others.

What you can do

● Talk to the parents or carers about what seem to be the triggers for their child's asthma and what steps you should take. Find out how the inhaler works.

● Children with asthma must have their reliever inhalers whenever they need them.

● It is helpful if the carers can give you a spare inhaler to keep in your setting.

● Keep a diary record which might help you to identify any other triggers in your setting. Record the child's symptoms and what you think might have set them off. Make sure that you share this daily with the family.

● Ensure that a child's reliever inhaler is always at hand and that it is used as soon as the child starts to cough, wheeze and become short of breath. The parents or carers may also advise you to use it *before* physical activity or other events which might trigger an attack.

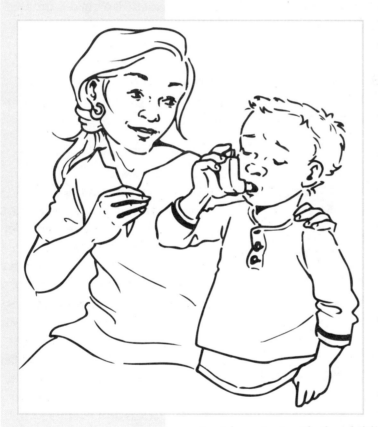

● Stay calm and reassure the child. Reliever inhalers usually work quickly to relax the muscles and allow normal breathing. Do not put your arm around their shoulder as this can restrict their breathing.

● Encourage the child to breathe slowly and deeply by breathing with them yourself. Loosen any tight clothing, sit down together and show the child how to lean slightly forwards if this helps.

● As soon as the attack is over, help the child to return to your normal activities.

● If the medication does not work after five to ten minutes, if the child is too distressed to talk or if you are worried about their condition, call an ambulance. The parents can tell you what would constitute an emergency in their child's case.

● Avoid contact with the child's known triggers as far as you are able. This might involve keeping your soft surfaces dust-free, keeping the child away from furry pets and taking general common-sense precautions against spreading coughs and colds.

Allergies

What are allergies?

Some children react to certain substances by producing a rash and runny eyes and nose, or developing breathing difficulties or changed behaviour. This is due to an altered immune response in their bodies. Hay fever, eczema and asthma are examples of allergic responses, though there are other ways in which a child might show an allergic response, which we will consider in this section.

The sorts of substances that children with allergies react to range widely. They might be things a child has inhaled, touched or taken into their body, such as pollen, dust mites, animals, penicillin, nuts (such as peanuts), foods, latex or certain chemicals.

An allergic condition can be very mild or extremely serious and life-threatening, as when a child goes into 'anaphylactic shock' and emergency help is needed immediately. It will depend on each individual child and the particular reaction they produce in response to the allergen. Allergic reactions might be delayed or might develop very quickly and obviously. These children are not infectious and an allergy cannot be 'caught' from anyone else.

Allergies can be difficult to identify and diagnose. Sometimes skin tests are used, or foods are eliminated from the child's diet to see what effect they have on the child.

All over the world, there is evidence that allergic diseases are increasing; approximately 10 to 20% of all school children have some form of allergy.

What you can do
● Ask parents and carers routinely about any allergies their children have when they first join you.
● Find out what this means for the child and for you. How serious is the reaction? What are the signs that you should look out for and at what stage should you take any special action? What foods or situations should be avoided?
● Look for a common-sense balance in keeping early years experiences as normal as possible, yet taking reasonable precautions to ensure that the child remains comfortable and safe.

● Ask the carers to explain to you when any medication should be used, to show you how to use any inhalers or sprays, and to tell you how much help their child needs with these. Follow your usual procedures for obtaining parental consent if you are required to help with medication.
● For children who have marked symptoms, or for those whose allergies are still being assessed, keep a diary to share with the parents or carers about what led up to a reaction, what the reaction was, and what happened as a result. This is useful for carers to share with the doctors involved.
● Keep your indoor space as free from dust as possible. Wash fabrics and cushions regularly and use non-allergenic covers and fabrics if possible.
● Make sure that you are confident about the ingredients in the food that

you provide. For some children, it is essential that they do not have even the smallest trace of an allergen such as a nut.

Diabetes
What is diabetes?

Diabetes is caused when there is not enough insulin produced in the body. Insulin is a hormone responsible for glucose metabolism and it helps us to store glucose, ready for when our body needs energy. There are approximately 15 to 20 children per 100,000 diagnosed with diabetes each year, and this is increasing.

Diabetes can start quite suddenly, for no known reason, and it can also be hereditary.

There are two forms of diabetes; one affecting children and young adults, and one starting in middle age. Most children have Type 1 or 'insulin-dependent diabetes mellitus', in which the insulin-producing cells of the pancreas have been destroyed.

The first symptoms that you might notice are excessive thirst, large amounts of urine being passed frequently, weight loss, irritability and tiredness, an unusual smell of pear drops to the breath and a reduced resistance to infections. Diabetes is diagnosed through a blood test and children are usually prescribed regular insulin injections to control their blood sugar. Many older children give themselves their injections and can also learn how to test their blood and urine sugar levels.

If the child's blood sugar level falls too low, this is called a hypoglycaemia episode, or 'hypo'.

What you can do

● Talk to the parents or carers about their child's regime. What special diet are they on? What signs will you see when the child's blood sugar has fallen too low and what should you do about it?
● Most parents will send in any snacks that might be necessary before the child does physical exercise. They might ask you to have a sugary drink on hand for their child at these times.
● Make sure that the child never misses a meal or snack time.
● Look out for a hypoglycaemia episode. Symptoms include hunger, sweating, drowsiness, pallor, glazed eyes, shaking, poor concentration and irritability.
● If the parents or carers need you to check their child's sugar levels and this has been agreed, ask them to show you how to use any special equipment.

● Let the parents or carers know when there are infections among children or staff in your setting; sometimes this will imply different insulin requirements.

● Many children who have diabetes have the condition under control and it should not affect your time together in your setting, apart from the need to look out for sugar 'lows'.

Epilepsy

What is epilepsy?

Some children have recurrent seizures or 'fits'. These are due to bursts of excessive electrical activity in the brain. Seizures can take many forms and vary from child to child. The type of seizure depends on the part of the brain in which these bursts start and spread to. About one person in two hundred is affected.

Sometimes a child has a seizure because of a very high temperature (known as a 'febrile convulsion'). Having a single seizure like this does not normally mean that the child has epilepsy.

Medical investigations can often lead to medication which will help to control the epilepsy. These children have to be monitored by the doctors as they grow older and their condition changes. The epilepsy will disappear for many children. Epilepsy is not a mental illness and is not infectious.

Some children have 'generalized seizures' in which their bodies stiffen, they may cry out, fall and then convulse. These last a few minutes usually and the child may be drowsy and disorientated

afterwards. Others may look blank, twitch slightly or blink for a few seconds. These may be difficult to spot if you are not familiar with the child. Other children may have 'myoclonic seizures' in which a limb or set of muscles jerks for a while, sometimes leading to a fall. Children can also experience 'partial seizures' in which they might repeat a behaviour or mannerism, wander or appear unresponsive. These last for 30 seconds to two minutes or so, and the child remains conscious. Though some children have more than one type of seizure, most will have just one type.

What you can do

● If a child has epilepsy, ask the parents or carers to describe what might happen and exactly what you should do about it. Ask them to stay with their child for the first few sessions to demonstrate if there are regular seizures. Ask if there is anything in particular which might trigger their attacks.

● Make sure that you know at what stage any emergency treatment should be called for – for example, if a seizure lasts two minutes longer than is usual for that child, or if the child begins to have another seizure before regaining consciousness from the first.

● If a child not known to have epilepsy has a seizure, this would also be a case for calling an ambulance.

● If a child is having a seizure, protect the child from injury by cushioning their head and placing them on their side so that they can breathe easily. Do not restrict their movements or give them anything to drink. Stay beside them until they have recovered.

● It might not be possible to have the child in a quiet area as you will need to handle the seizure where it happens. Instead, ask a helper to calmly reassure the other children and draw them away to another activity, leaving you to await the recovery quietly.

● If a child is having a partial seizure, lead them gently away from any danger and talk quietly to reassure them.

● If a child's epilepsy is currently being assessed and diagnosed by a paediatrician or neurologist, you might be able to help by keeping a diary of seizures or unusual mannerisms. Write down when they took place, what happened, what you did and how quickly the child recovered. A diary will also help you to monitor the effects of any new medication.

HIV and AIDS

What are HIV and AIDS?

AIDS is caused by a virus called HIV (Human Immunodeficiency Virus) which can damage the body's defence system against certain infections. Blood tests can be used to detect whether a person is 'HIV-positive' (carrying the HIV virus). People who are HIV-positive may go on to develop AIDS at some point, though the time-scale is variable. It is transmitted through unprotected sexual intercourse, through injecting with infected needles and from an infected mother to an unborn child. There were about 600 babies born with HIV in this country between 1989 and 1999, of whom just over half developed AIDS by 1999 and a quarter died. Improved medication has helped greatly to improve the life expectancy of babies born to HIV-positive mothers. Many live to six years or more before experiencing illness. Antenatal tests for HIV are now generally offered as a matter of course in high-risk areas.

Most school-age children with HIV will have been told that 'there is something in their blood' and they tend to instinctively keep this secret. Younger children are not likely to know that there is anything wrong unless they become ill.

Children with HIV pose little risk to others, though they may themselves be prone to dangerous infections from others. There is no evidence that HIV can be transmitted by everyday social contact, such as cuddles, coughs, sneezes, tears, saliva or sharing a toilet seat.

You may not be told that a child has HIV, though many parents tell at least one member of staff so that they can be alerted about particular infections in the setting.

What you can do

● Take sensible precautions whenever dealing with bleeding incidents for *all* children. Wear protective gloves and dispose of all products safely.

● Normal everyday standards of good hygiene are quite sufficient.

● Follow the first aid and health and safety guidelines of your particular setting or Authority.

● Maintain confidentiality; parents are under no obligation to tell you that their child has HIV. Operate a 'need to know' policy in your setting.

● Make sure that colleagues are sensibly informed about HIV and AIDS so that they can avoid any over-reaction or feelings of rejection.

● Warn parents and carers about any virulent infections going around, such as chicken pox.

● Remember that the carers might be particularly in need of your support and understanding.

● Build up a resource library for colleagues and carers so that everyone becomes better informed about the condition. Share accurate information and try to expel any myths and misunderstandings.

Cancer and leukaemia

What are cancer and leukaemia?

In a cancer, certain cells multiply too quickly. Sometimes a tumour is formed, perhaps in the brain or the bowel. Some cancers do affect children and the most common is leukaemia.

Leukaemia is a rare form of cancer affecting the white blood cells. Children become anaemic, their blood does not clot properly and they cannot fight infections well. So the first symptoms are increased bruising, infection and tiredness. You might also see recurrent nose bleeds and a purplish rash, and the child might complain that their joints are painful.

The outlook for children with leukaemia is now so much better than it used to be, with at least 50% being completely cured. However, the child might need to spend a considerable amount of time in hospital or receiving treatment.

What you can do

● If you are worried about a child's symptoms, have a quiet word with the parents or health visitor, so that they can be medically checked.
● Keep closely in touch with the child's family and help to keep up the morale of family, siblings and friends while the child is away.
● Look for ways of keeping your links with a child who is in hospital (you will find plenty of ideas in Chapters 4 to 9).
● When a child is being treated or is still convalescing, warn the carers if there are any infectious diseases such as chicken pox in the setting.

Meningitis

What is meningitis?

'Meningitis' literally means 'inflammation of the meninges', the meninges being the membrane lining the brain and the spinal cord. Meningitis can be caused by different kinds of germs, and its level of seriousness depends on the germ involved.

Bacterial meningitis is quite rare, with around 2,000 reported cases per year in the UK. However, it can be very serious and needs urgent treatment with antibiotics.

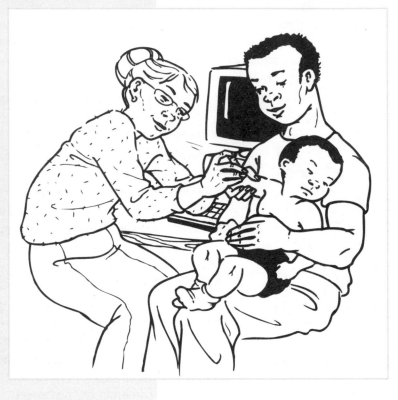

Viral meningitis is more common and is rarely life-threatening, though it can make the sufferer feel very weak and poorly. Antibiotics are not effective with viral meningitis, so this is usually treated with nursing, rest and care. The germs that cause bacterial meningitis live naturally in the back of the nose and throat. People of any age can be carrying these germs, and it is only rarely that the body's defences become overwhelmed by them and an infection like meningitis develops. The germs can be spread by coughing, sneezing and very close contact, but do not survive for long outside the body. They are not likely to be passed through toys and equipment, though good hygiene practice, especially with mouthed toys, should always be followed.

The most common form of infant bacterial meningitis used to be the Hib bacterium. From October 1992, routine immunisation with Hib vaccine was introduced for babies. This has dramatically reduced the number of cases, particularly in the first year of life. Children over four rarely develop Hib meningitis. The vaccine only works for this particular kind of meningitis. Other bacterial forms, meningococcal and pneumococcal, cannot yet be immunized against.

The symptoms are: a fever, vomiting, headache, and a marked stiffness, particularly at the back of the neck; the child turns away from any bright light, might complain of joint stiffness, and, in time,

becomes drowsy and dull. Sometimes they develop fits and a widespread blotchy rash or bruising associated with blood poisoning, or septicaemia. The illness sometimes develops over one or two days, but can come on very quickly, in a matter of a few hours. In these cases, it becomes clear quickly that the child is very ill and emergency treatment should be sought.

Recovering from meningitis can take time, and nine out of ten sufferers of bacterial meningitis are successfully treated in hospital.

What you can do
● Make sure that you and your colleagues are aware of the symptoms of meningitis and take immediate action if you suspect that a child might be affected.
● Children who are recovering from viral meningitis can feel weak, debilitated and depressed for some time afterwards. They may feel floppy, tired and irritable, and might need your patience and reassurance for several weeks.
● If they have spent time in hospital, this too will take some time to adjust to, particularly if treatment was unpleasant and frightening. Do not be concerned if the child needs more cuddles and attention than usual, can only manage a short session at pre-school, or resorts to a younger 'baby' stage for a while.
● All people recovering from meningitis might find that they feel tired, giddy, forgetful and moody for several weeks afterwards.
● You might find that new skills learned in pre-school have been lost and need re-teaching.

● You might see more temper tantrums than usual, or perhaps a very short concentration span.
● Keep a particular note of the child's hearing since this may well have been affected and need an up-to-date check.
● Just occasionally, there are longer-term and serious complications, leading to learning difficulties, behaviour difficulties, epilepsy or problems in hearing and seeing. It is important to stress that these effects are rare.
● Your own records of how the child is playing and behaving in your setting will give important information about any long-term effects the illness might have had.

Cystic fibrosis
What is cystic fibrosis?
Some children are born with a condition called 'cystic fibrosis'. It is the most common inherited disorder among Caucasians in the UK today. It affects about one in 2,000 children. For these children, the mucous glands produce abnormally thick, sticky

mucus, and their sweat glands produce excess salt. Though their lungs will have been normal at birth, each time the children have an infection this sticky mucus collects in the lungs and blocks airways causing further damage. All infections therefore need careful treatment. The pancreas will be affected too. The small channels which normally allow enzymes to flow into the intestine become blocked, leading to cysts. These children therefore need to take digestive enzymes orally at each mealtime.

Children with cystic fibrosis have daily physiotherapy. The physiotherapist or carer claps the child's chest as he or she lies in different positions to help drain the mucus from various parts of the lungs. The child is then encouraged to cough productively.

What you can do

● Talk with the parents or carers to make sure that you have everything you need to know about their child's condition. Children may be affected differently, so this is important to know.

● Make sure that the child leads as normal a life as possible. Apart from having physiotherapy, taking enzymes and doing exercise every day, that child should be able to do what most children their age can do. Your task is to make them feel like everyone else.

● On hot days, you may need to remind the child to take extra salt. The parents will let you know what to do and when.

● If you are together at mealtimes, then the child will need to take regular enzymes. If they do not, they will begin to feel tired, get stomach ache, and need to go to the toilet a lot.

● Occasionally, children need their 'physio' at certain times of day, and so you might need to think how to do this discreetly.

● Expect the child to be absent from time to time with check-ups or when they are fighting infections.

● Have a quiet area that the child can settle into if they are feeling tired.

● Encourage physical exercise; again, the parents will tell you how much exercise their child should be getting each day. Exercise helps the lungs to stay fitter.

● Keep parents and carers informed of any infections going around. Though most children with CF are encouraged to keep attending, additional antibiotics might be needed.

● Ask the parents or carers about their child's diet – while certain foods are definitely encouraged, others might be less good for their child's health.

● Be reassured that if a child with cystic fibrosis coughs persistently, it is not infectious.

PERSONAL, SOCIAL AND EMOTIONAL DEVELOPMENT

The ideas in this chapter show how to keep in touch with a child who is away or in hospital, and suggest how to help children who have been absent to settle back into the group.

Meet my friend

LEARNING OBJECTIVE FOR ALL THE CHILDREN
● to be sensitive to the needs, views and feelings of others.

INDIVIDUAL LEARNING TARGET
● to feel welcome and included after a prolonged period of absence.

Group size
Six to ten children.

What you need
A large cuddly toy or giant puppet such as a dog.

What to do
This activity is especially helpful if there is a child in your group who has been away for a period of time and who has just begun to settle back with you again.

Gather the children in a circle, sitting on the floor. Introduce your cuddly toy to them, saying, for example, 'This is Lucie and she has come to play with you today, but she's *very* shy!'. Make Lucie cuddle into you, taking little peeps at the children. Stroke her head and reassure her by telling her, for example, 'Don't worry, Lucie, these very nice children will all help to look after you'.

Ask the children for ideas about helping Lucie feel at home. What could they show her? What would they play with? Make Lucie 'whisper' in your ear from time to time: 'Yes, Lucie says she'd like a story. Thank you'. She can then whisper to you that she would like to play with the child who has been away. Encourage the child to take Lucie with them to the story area to play.

Special support
While the child is still settling in, keep the size of the group small. This activity helps to boost the esteem of a child who is still feeling insecure within the group. It can also help them to play the role of a carer if they have been in the position of being cared for by others for the past few weeks. Finally, Lucie can herself become a comforter and security item for a child who is unsure of themselves or feeling unwell.

Extension
Pretend that Lucie has just come out of hospital. Use role-play to talk about and act out what happens in hospital.

LINKS WITH HOME
Allow an insecure child to take Lucie home with them for the night, or 'invite' her to go with them to the next clinic or hospital appointment.

Bear's headache

Group size
The whole group.

What you need
A large teddy bear.

What to do
Sit together in a circle. Introduce this song which can be sung to the tune of 'John Brown's Body' (Traditional):

> Poor old Teddy's got a pain inside his head (x3)
> So he went to see the doctor who sent him straight to bed!

(Invite different children to rub the part of Teddy which is hurting.)

> Poor old Teddy's got an ache inside his tummy (x3)
> So we had to keep him quiet while we telephoned his mummy!

(Invite all the children to rub their own tummies if they are not rubbing Teddy's.)

> Poor old Teddy's got a burning in his chest (x3)
> So he had to go to hospital and stay in bed to rest!
>
> Poor old Teddy's got a cramp inside his leg (x3)
> So we rubbed it very hard until the pain had gone away!
>
> *Hannah Mortimer*

Make up other verses introducing new body parts and new words to describe painful feelings.

Special support
Very young children sometimes lack the words to describe what they feel like when they are ill. Choose body parts and use words that might be helpful for any child who has a medical condition. Let them help to look after Teddy in the game and rub the affected area.

Extension
Continue with an activity on hospitals, at the doctor's or in bed, making Teddy feel better.

LEARNING OBJECTIVE FOR ALL THE CHILDREN
● to understand that people have different needs.

INDIVIDUAL LEARNING TARGET
● to develop vocabulary relating to body parts.

LINKS WITH HOME
Ask parents and carers to talk with their children about any friend, relative or neighbour who is unwell, and to help them think of ways of making the person feel happier (perhaps sending them a 'get well' card or visiting them).

LEARNING OBJECTIVES FOR ALL THE CHILDREN
● to respond to significant experiences
● to be sensitive to the needs, views and feelings of others.

INDIVIDUAL LEARNING TARGET
● to maintain relationships with the children and adults in the setting.

Thinking of you

Group size
Two or three children at a time.

What you need
A scrapbook with one page for each child in your group (or make your own from folded A3 sheets of coloured sugar paper); glue; scissors; felt-tipped pens; white paper.

What to do
This activity is suitable for when one of the children is in hospital or poorly at home for a length of time. Use group or circle time to talk with all the children about where the child is. Explain that they will be away for a long time and so they will miss their friends and all the activities that you do in the group.

Ask the children for ideas about how you might keep in touch with the child while they are away. Talk about letters and cards, and lead on to suggesting that the children write a book all about what they are doing to send to their friend in hospital. Show the children the scrapbook and invite each of them to draw a picture and tell you what they would like you to write. Decide on a title page together, such as 'Carly's book, from your friends at nursery'.

Sit down with two or three children at a time, encouraging them to draw something that they have enjoyed in your group on a sheet of white paper. Glue it on to one page of the scrapbook. Then ask them what they would like you to write to Carly. Write this on another small sheet of paper and mount it on the same page. Invite each child in the group to fill one page of the scrapbook.

Special support
Send the book to the parents or carers so that it can be taken into hospital and read to their child.

Extension
Older children may be able to write or copy their own sentences.

LINKS WITH HOME
Ask the parents or carers to let you know when their child is ready for you to send a few activities into hospital for them.

LEARNING OBJECTIVE FOR ALL THE CHILDREN
● to form good relationships with adults and peers.

INDIVIDUAL LEARNING TARGET
● to identify with a group of children and feel included.

Holding hands

Group size
Ten to 20 children.

What you need
The photocopiable sheet on page 86; long non-slip strip of carpet.

What to do
Stand up in a circle and introduce the song as you hold hands and walk around in a circle. The song fits the tune of the traditional nursery rhyme 'Girls and Boys Come Out to Play'. Adapt the words to suit the children in the group, for example, asking, 'Who comes to school with Gran?', 'Who comes with their big sister?', 'Who comes with their childminder? What is her name?'.

Now ask the children to choose a partner and hold hands as you march around the room, singing the song. Then suggest that you make a 'road'. Lay the strip of carpet down and, as partners approach the 'road', encourage them to look each way before crossing. Are there any cars coming? If the weather is fine, you can take the song outside into your road play area.

Special support
This is a helpful action rhyme for encouraging children to hold hands and relate to a partner or group of friends. It can be used as a 'warming-up' activity if you are supporting a child who is settling back into the group following a long absence. Ask them quietly who they would like to have as their partner, and stay close to reassure them if needed.

Extension
Look for other action rhymes and movement games that involve partners and touch, such as 'Row, Row, Row Your Boat' (Traditional). Follow this activity by introducing some basic road safety guidance.

LINKS WITH HOME
Send home a copy of the photocopiable sheet so that parents and carers can chant it as they hold their children's hands and walk home.

Five currant buns

Group size
Eleven to 24 children.

What you need
Card; felt-tipped pens; scissors; small strips of Velcro; strong glue (adult use).

What to do
Start by inviting five children to help you make the currant buns from card. Prepare a card headband for each child (see diagram, right), adding a 'currant bun' on the front and sticking a strip of Velcro at either end to make the headband adjustable. This will hold it in place on the child's forehead and you will be able to reuse your 'props'. Help each child to cut out their headband and invite them to colour it in.

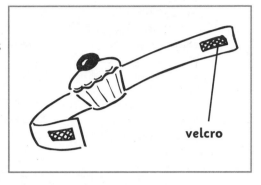

velcro

When the glue has dried, gather the children in a circle, sitting on the floor. Invite the five children who made the 'buns' to stand up wearing their headbands. Then chant or sing this traditional rhyme:

Five currant buns in a baker's shop,
Round and fat with a cherry on the top.
Along came a boy with a penny one day,
Bought a currant bun and took it away.

Invite another child to come and choose a 'bun', pretending to pay you a penny and leading the 'bun' back to their place. Substitute that child's name for 'a boy' in the verse. Repeat for 'Four currant buns...' and so on. By the end of the song, you will have new children sitting next to each other and you can repeat the song with new 'buns'!

Special support
Include a child who has been absent for a while as one of the 'buns'. Follow the song up with an activity in which the children have to work in pairs, so that the child continues to be supported by their new friend.

Extension
Challenge older children to make props for some of your other favourite songs, such as 'Five (Ten) Green Bottles', 'Five Little Speckled Frogs' or 'Miss Polly Had a Dolly'.

LEARNING OBJECTIVE FOR ALL THE CHILDREN
● to form good relationships with peers.

INDIVIDUAL LEARNING TARGET
● to make friends again quickly after an absence.

LINKS WITH HOME
Ask parents and carers of newcomers whether their children have any friends already in the group. You can then partner them together for extra support.

LEARNING OBJECTIVE FOR ALL THE CHILDREN
● to understand that they can expect others to treat their needs and views with respect.

INDIVIDUAL LEARNING TARGET
● to feel positive about themselves.

Knotted up

Group size
12 to 30 children.

What you need
A length of soft rope (about 1cm in diameter) long enough to go right around the inside of a circle of children; extra adult helpers; musical tape or CD; tape recorder or CD player.

What to do
Tie the ends of the rope together with a reef knot (right over left and under, left over right and under).

Sit in a circle and show the children how to hold on to the rope with two hands and how to pass it gently along by moving your hands apart and together. This is easier if you have adult helpers every four or five children. Play music as you encourage the children to pass the rope between them, and ask them to stop when the music stops.

When the music has stopped, chant:

> Who's got the knot?
> Who's got the knot?
> We'd like to know your name because
> We like you such a lot!
>
> *Hannah Mortimer*

Find out who is holding the knot. Now encourage the children and adults to join in saying why they like that person, for example, 'I like Mrs Thompson's smile!' or 'I like playing with Rashid on the bikes'.

Special support
Think of some comments that you can make about how well a child is settling back or how brave they were in hospital.

Extension
Introduce some sentence-completion activities into circle time, saying, for example, 'I like playing with Siok because…' or 'I am unhappy when…'.

LINKS WITH HOME
If two children particularly like playing with each other and one is absent for a length of time, ask the parents or carers if the friends can 'write' to each other, and to support them as they do this.

Tear bottle

Group size
One child at a time.

What you need
A small precious bottle and stopper, such as an old perfume bottle.

What to do
If a child in your group is continuously tearful, there are various approaches that you can try. The most useful is distraction. Move quickly into an activity which is going to distract and interest the child so that they 'forget' to cry. Even for children who feel constantly unwell, distraction can be used to occupy and lift them out of themselves for a few minutes at a time. Keep the activities calming and reassuring.

For other children, you can talk to them and encourage them to be brave. Use stickers and smiley faces to praise them when you notice that they are not crying.

Some children become upset because they do not understand the routine. They constantly ask, 'Is it time for home yet?'. Sometimes a simple picture timetable showing what they are going to do next will help to reassure them. For example, you could say, 'First we play outside, then it is story time, then drinks, then free play, then music. After that, Dad comes to collect you'.

Other children use tears to seek attention, or cry almost out of habit. Reach for your precious bottle and commiserate: 'How sad you are today. Your tears are very precious and we must collect them for Granny. Can you see how many you can squeeze into this bottle?'. Miraculously, their eyes will begin to dry!

Special support
This is a clever way of reducing tearfulness when you feel that you have tried everything else. It comes from a Family Therapy approach and is a form of 'paradoxical injunction'.

Extension
Make a teardrop mobile by cutting drop shapes out of reflective card. Hang it over your quiet area to take the tears away.

LEARNING OBJECTIVE FOR ALL THE CHILDREN
● to have a developing awareness of their own feelings.

INDIVIDUAL LEARNING TARGET
● to be comforted or distracted when distressed and tearful.

LINKS WITH HOME
Share these ideas with families if they seem to help. Many children stop crying as soon as their parents or carers have left. However, you may need to reassure carers that this is the case as it can be difficult for them to believe.

PERSONAL, SOCIAL & EMOTIONAL DEVELOPMENT

LEARNING OBJECTIVE FOR ALL THE CHILDREN
● to have a developing awareness of the needs and feelings of others.

INDIVIDUAL LEARNING TARGET
● to feel able to talk about their medical difficulties if they need to.

Ted has diabetes

Group size
Six to ten children

What you need
Information about a medical condition such as diabetes; if available, a story-book associated with the condition (see page 95).

What to do
Sit down together on cushions and introduce Ted. Help Ted say 'Hello' to all the children and then make him whisper something to you. Explain to the children that Ted has been to see the doctor and has found out that he has a condition called diabetes. Ask the children if they know anything about diabetes and encourage any child with the condition, if they choose, to talk about it.

Introduce a story-book to read to Ted, such as *I'm Tougher Than Diabetes* by Althea (Happy Cat Books). Make Teddy look very interested and whisper to you how good it is to know that other children have diabetes too. Encourage the children to ask Ted questions, for example, 'Is the condition catching?', 'Will it go away?', 'Do the injections hurt?' and so on. Use your own knowledge to answer.

Special support
Choose a condition that might be personally relevant to a child in, or soon to join, your group. Do not tell the children that a child has that condition, though they themselves might volunteer information. You can follow up the group activity by talking individually with the child about their condition if it is helpful.

Extension
If you do not know an answer to a question, suggest that you find it out together. There are useful addresses on page 94.

LINKS WITH HOME
When you collect basic medical information about the children, ask the parents or carers of a child who has a condition what he or she understands about it as well.

COMMUNICATION, LANGUAGE AND LITERACY

These activities encourage the development of children's language and literacy skills while keeping an absent child in touch with the group. They provide natural opportunities for reading, writing and talking.

Mail box

Group size
Three or four children at a time.

What you need
Letter paper; envelopes; selection of felt-tipped pens and pencils.

What to do
This activity can be introduced when one of the children is away from the group due to hospital or medical treatment, or illness. Gather everyone together and talk about the child who is missing. Point out that you have not seen them for a while; does anyone know where they are? Some of the children might know the child personally and this will provide you with some information about which children are still in touch. Explain in simple terms what is happening concerning the child. Try to encourage the children to think about what the child might be feeling. Then talk about the people who help to make us feel better. Ask the children to think about what it must be like not to see their friends or be able to play with them. What do they think they could do to help?

Suggest a letter-writing activity. Work in small groups to draw pictures, and write down what the children want the letter to say. Have a separate letter from each child and encourage them to sign their name at whichever level they can manage. Place each letter in its own envelope and encourage the children to write or copy the child's name on the front and stick down the flap.

When you are gathered together again, make a ceremony of sealing all the small envelopes into one large one and writing on the address of the child who is away.

Special support
This activity will help the absent child to keep in touch with their friends and playmates in your group.

Extension
Encourage older children to write their own short letters, with your help if necessary.

LEARNING OBJECTIVES FOR ALL THE CHILDREN
● to know that print carries meaning
● to attempt writing for various purposes.

INDIVIDUAL LEARNING TARGET
● to hear about what the children have been doing at nursery, pre-school or school.

LINKS WITH HOME
Encourage parents and carers to help their children write a real letter to a relative or friend and post it to them.

LEARNING OBJECTIVE FOR ALL THE CHILDREN
● to attempt writing a 'prescription'.

INDIVIDUAL LEARNING TARGET
● to have the opportunity to talk about medicines.

Miss Polly

Group size
Six to ten children.

What you need
A girl doll; doctor's kit (toy stethoscope, medical case, hat and so on); toy bed; paper; pencils.

What to do
Sit together in a circle on the floor. Introduce the familiar and traditional rhyme 'Miss Polly Had a Dolly' in *This Little Puffin...* compiled by Elizabeth Matterson (Puffin Books).

Repeat the song as you carry out actions, miming Miss Polly rocking the baby and telephoning, then miming the doctor's bag and hat, rapping and writing. Repeat the song with role-play and props, and ask the children to volunteer to take it in turns to be Miss Polly and the doctor.

After a few turns, exclaim that you do not have any paper saying what the doctor has written down! Introduce the word 'prescription' and talk about medicines and how they help us. Give each child a piece of paper and pencil and ask them to go away and make a prescription for the doctor to give Miss Polly. Gather together again to admire everybody's work and sing the song once more with your new props.

Special support
This activity could lead on to a more detailed and individual talk about medicines, if this would help the child.

Extension
Encourage the children to think through what a prescription should say: the name of the medicine, who it is for and how often to take it.

LINKS WITH HOME
If you are issuing medicines in your setting, make sure that you have read through Chapter I and considered your policy.

LEARNING OBJECTIVE FOR ALL THE CHILDREN

● to show an understanding of the elements of stories.

INDIVIDUAL LEARNING TARGET

● to enjoy a story in hospital or at home.

Story kit

Group size
Four to six children.

What you need
A well-known story such as 'Little Red Riding Hood' (Traditional) and various props to go with it; small cardboard box; card; felt-tipped pens or crayons; scissors.

What to do
In this activity, the children put together a 'story kit' with props for a child who is spending time at home or in hospital. This is a very similar idea to 'story sacks' but the aim is to make the kit smaller and manageable for a child in bed.

Gather the children together and talk about the child who is unwell and what might help. Suggest that they might really enjoy a story. Invite the children to think of one – for example, 'Little Red Riding Hood' – and then plan how to make it really interesting.

Read the chosen story through with all the children and decide together what props you will collect. Have you got a tiny doll who could be 'Red Riding Hood'? Have you got a Granny doll? Can the children find one of the zoo animals to be Mr Wolf? You could make a woodcutter out of card! In this way, keep all the children busy as they look around for useful props for the story. Aim to get all the props into a small cardboard box. Decorate the box by sticking on a picture of the story and adding the title, and send it to the child who is away.

Special support
Send the story-book along with the box of props, or write your own simplified version for a parent or carer to read to the absent child. You can add side notes to refer to your props, for example, 'Look for Mr Woodcutter in your box'.

Extension
Older children can create a whole kit on their own, with your support.

LINKS WITH HOME
Lend the story and the kit to parents and carers to share with their children at home or, for a sick child, in hospital.

LEARNING OBJECTIVES FOR ALL THE CHILDREN
● to use talk to organize, sequence and clarify thinking and ideas
● to attempt writing for various purposes.

INDIVIDUAL LEARNING TARGET
● to feel included while absent from the setting.

Message in a bottle

Group size
Four to six children.

What you need
An empty plastic bottle (such as a lemonade bottle); A4 sheet of good-quality paper; felt-tipped pens.

What to do
This activity can lead on from a general discussion about helping an absent child to keep in touch. It also links well into a topic on pirates or messages.

Invent a story about a teddy who was shipwrecked on a beautiful island, for example:

> Teddy began to get very hungry and missed his family a great deal. So he wrote a message – 'Come and rescue me – I'm on the island with the rock shaped like an ice-cream cone!'. He rolled it tightly and placed it in an old bottle, pushing the cork in to keep it dry. Ten days later, his bottle was found by a little boy at the seaside. He told his parents and soon the rescue ship was on its way.

Suggest that you all make a message in a bottle to send to the child who is away. Say that the message could tell the child all about what you have been doing in your setting.

Work together at a table to fill your sheet with contributions from all the children, adding your own commentaries. Roll it carefully and put it in the bottle, so that the edge can be reached and retrieved easily.

Special support
Your commentaries can tell the child about everything you have been doing in your setting and what you are planning to do once the child is back with you.

Extension
Older children can make their own messages in bottles. Make the messages look old and mysterious by adding glue to the edges and rubbing in sand.

LINKS WITH HOME
Ask another child and their parent or carer if they could deliver the message so that they can keep in touch too.

LEARNING OBJECTIVE FOR ALL THE CHILDREN
● to use language to imagine and re-create roles and experiences.

INDIVIDUAL LEARNING TARGET
● to listen to and enjoy a story, even if feeling unwell.

Glove stories

Group size
Two or three children.

What you need
A picture book of a familiar story such as 'The Three Billy Goats Gruff' (Traditional); old woollen glove; coloured felt squares; fabric glue and a needle and thread for yourself.

What to do
Gather together for your story and enjoy the pictures. Explain that you would like to lend the story to a child who is ill in bed. Say that the child is feeling very poorly at the moment and that to cheer them up you would like to make the story as interesting as possible. Suggest that it would be good to make some finger puppets to go with the story. Decide who your characters are going to be – perhaps the three Billy Goats and the troll.

Now move to a table and use the children's ideas to cut out and stick tiny faces on to the fingertips of the glove (see illustration above). Later, add a few stitches to make sure that the glove puppets stay in position.

Special support
Send the story-book and the glove to the child who is ill for a quiet story that they can enjoy from their bed.

Extension
Older children can make their own finger puppets to go with the story.

LINKS WITH HOME
Take a moment to show the parents or carers of the sick child what you have made with the children and how the finger puppets relate to the story. Suggest that their child might like to wear the glove and move the characters. The other parents might like to try this activity at home too.

LEARNING OBJECTIVES FOR ALL THE CHILDREN
● to use talk to organize, sequence and clarify thinking
● to know that print carries meaning and, in English, is read from left to right and top to bottom.

INDIVIDUAL LEARNING TARGET
● to feel included in the group's news when absent.

LINKS WITH HOME
Before this activity, ask the parents and carers of all the children to send in some holiday postcards that they have received. Afterwards, ask them to help their children post the cards that they have made.

From me to you

Group size
Three or four children at a time.

What you need
A selection of holiday postcards; sheets of card cut to postcard size; waterproof felt-tipped pens; postage stamps; aprons.

What to do
This is a postcard designing and writing session to stay in touch with a child who is absent.

Share the postcards with the children and talk about why we send postcards and why it is fun to receive them. Look at how the writing is on one side and the picture on the other. See where the stamp goes. Why do we have to put stamps on before we post postcards and letters?

Introduce the idea that one of the children is away at the moment. Suggest that it would be a good idea to make your own postcards to keep in touch.

Help the children to put on aprons. Explain to them that the pens that they will be using do not wash off – in this way, the writing will not run off when it rains. Support each child as they illustrate one side of the card and help them to say what they want on the other side, perhaps with you writing or helping them to copy. They should add their name and stick on real stamps.

Special support
The children could also make a postcard for the child who is away to send back. Stamp it and address it to 'The Children of…' (your setting). The absent child could then add his or her own message with help.

Extension
Talk about the postcards that you have collected and the countries that they have come from.

SPECIAL NEEDS **in the early years:** Medical difficulties

COMMUNICATION, LANGUAGE & LITERACY

LEARNING OBJECTIVES FOR ALL THE CHILDREN
● to write their own names
● to use language to predict.

INDIVIDUAL LEARNING TARGET
● to feel included in the group when absent.

LINKS WITH HOME
Ask parents and carers to spend a few minutes before bed enjoying a lift-the-flap book with their children and encouraging them to talk about what is coming next.

Which animal is this?

Group size
Whole group, four children at a time.

What you need
A copy of *Flappy Waggy Wiggly* by Amanda Leslie (Little Tiger Press); sugar-paper scrapbook made out of A3 sheets folded into an A4 book and stapled together, with one double page for each child; white paper; glue stick; pencils; scissors; washable felt-tipped pens.

What to do
Start by sharing the lift-the-flap book *Flappy Waggy Wiggly* with all the children. This is a colourful book which has an animal hidden under a flap on each page, with just the tip of its nose and tail tantalizingly showing. On the flap is a description of that animal. Can the children guess what each animal is? Lift the flap and share their pleasure.

Now suggest that you make your own lift-the-flap book all about the children in your group. Invite four children at a time to a table. Ask each child to draw a picture of themselves and write their name beside it. Help them to cut around their picture and stick it on to a right-side page of the scrapbook. Cut out a flap of contrasting sugar paper, large enough to fit over their picture with just the tips showing. Hinge one side and glue the hinge on to the scrapbook.

Help each child to give you some words to describe themselves and write questions, using these words, on the front of the flap – for example, 'Who has dark hair, wears a purple sari and loves singing?'.

Gradually build up your lift-the-flap book and enjoy it together.

Special support
This is a lovely book to share with a member of your group who is absent or in hospital. Leave a page to include their own picture in the middle of the book.

Extension
Provide support to older children while they make their own lift-the-flap animal books.

LEARNING OBJECTIVE FOR ALL THE CHILDREN
● to use language to imagine and re-create experiences.

INDIVIDUAL LEARNING TARGET
● to act out feelings associated with hospitals and medical care.

LINKS WITH HOME
If a child's play reveals that they are anxious about an impending visit to hospital, talk to their parents or carers. Ask all the parents to point out the local hospital to their children at the next opportunity.

Small world

Group size
All the children, at different times.

What you need
A hospital play set.

What to do
Set up a corner with the hospital equipment. Set it up carefully, perhaps before the children arrive. Decide how many children can play with the toys at any one time and put up a sign saying '4 can play' with four children's outlines.

The most productive small-world play usually follows on from a stimulus story or play session. Start the activity by reading the children a story about going to hospital, such as *Hospital* by Althea (Happy Cat Books) or by playing alongside the children to get the game going. Continue to join in for a while but take your lead from what the children want you to do. Use your commentary, for example, 'Why is she looking so upset now?', to extend their thinking and to aid their understanding. Do not be surprised if the play takes on all kinds of new directions! If you end up having mass pile-ups on the roads, use your intervention to help the children act through 'helping' and 'rescue' roles!

Special support
Use your small-world toys to play individually with a child who has recently experienced hospital or is soon to visit one. The play may reveal how much they understand about their condition and what is going to happen to them. It will give you an opportunity for reassuring and providing information at a level they can cope with and understand.

Extension
After the hospital visit, make your own 'I'm going to hospital' book with the child ready to reassure the next visitor from your group.

MATHEMATICAL DEVELOPMENT

These activities show how you can continue to teach early maths skills to children who are unwell. There are plenty of ideas for using number rhymes and for enjoying maths activities for children who have to stay in bed.

Doctor, doctor

Group size
Eight to 12 children.

What you need
A toy medicine bottle and spoon; medicine bag; set of ten postcard-size cards, each with one number on, 1 to 10.

What to do
Gather the children in a circle, sitting on the floor. Show the children the pretend medicine and place it in the bag in the centre of the circle. Talk about medicines. Explain that you should never take any unless the doctor says so.

Show the children the ten cards in order from 1 to 10 and encourage them to call out each number as you show it. Then place the cards number-side down on the floor. Turn over one number at a time and challenge the children to call out what you have turned over. Introduce this chant:

> Doctor, doctor, please be quick
> (Simon's) not well and he might be sick!

Let the children take it in turns to be the doctor and stand in the circle holding the bag as the children chant. Substitute a child's name in the second line. Then ask a third child to turn over one of the number cards and to say what number it is. Next, say, 'Doctor, please give Simon *four* spoonfuls of medicine' (or whatever number was turned over). Support the 'doctor' as he or she counts out and gives the 'patient' four spoonfuls, one at a time, with all the children counting out loud together. Repeat for new children and new cards.

Special support
For younger children, start with three to five cards.

Extension
Lead on to talking more about medicines and pills. Emphasize the safety rules clearly.

LEARNING OBJECTIVES FOR ALL THE CHILDREN
- to count reliably up to ten
- to recognize numerals to 10.

INDIVIDUAL LEARNING TARGET
- to feel confident and reassured when role-playing 'doctors and patients'.

LINKS WITH HOME
Tell parents and carers that you have been talking about medicines and pills and that you have explained to the children that they should never take any which the doctor has not prescribed. Suggest that parents keep medicines locked away from children.

LEARNING OBJECTIVES FOR ALL THE CHILDREN
● to use language such as 'more' or 'less'
● to count reliably up to five.

INDIVIDUAL LEARNING TARGET
● to have the opportunity to talk about medication and treatment.

LINKS WITH HOME
Ask parents and carers to help you save up packaging for this activity.

At the chemist's

Group size
Two to four children at a time.

What you need
Items to create a chemist's shop, such as empty shampoo bottles, face-cream pots, toothpaste boxes, medicine boxes, photographic film boxes, sun-glasses, make-up or face-paints, empty perfume bottles and so on; table; plastic hand-held mirror; toy cash register and money; shopping baskets; paper bags; price labels; felt-tipped pen.

What to do
This is a different idea for your shop corner. Arrange the shop products imaginatively and place the mirror handy for admiring make-up or trying on sun-glasses. Label all the products from 1p to 5p.

Start by talking to everybody about the different activities that they can choose from today. Introduce the chemist's shop. Can anyone think of what you can buy from a chemist's? Encourage the children as they think of plenty of ideas.

Now help the children to take it in turns to play in the shop and to develop their own roles. One might be the shop assistant advising on the make-up, one might be the dispenser, handing out the medicines, one might be a sales assistant on the till and one might be a customer. Encourage the children to hand out money and to count coins as they make their purchases.

Special support
If one of the children has recently had to take a lot of medication, this activity might help them to talk about it and their condition. It might also help them to make their experiences more natural and part of everyday life. For younger children, have everything priced at 1p or 2p, and use 1p coins only.

Extension
For older children, use real money with 1p, 2p, 5p and 10p coins.

LEARNING OBJECTIVE FOR ALL THE CHILDREN
● to recognize numerals 1 to 10.

INDIVIDUAL LEARNING TARGET
● to be involved in a gentle number activity even if feeling weak or in bed.

1, 2, 3, 4, 5!

Group size
One poorly child.

What you need
An old woollen glove; coloured felt discs (about 1.5cm in diameter); needle, thread and marker pen (all for adult use).

What to do
Make yourself a 'number glove' by stitching felt discs on to the fingertips of an old pair of gloves. Stretchy gloves are excellent because they fit adults as well as children (stitch the felt in the centre so that it does not matter when the glove stretches). On to each disc of felt, write the numerals 1 to 5 using the marker pen.

Show the child the glove and wave your fingers. Invite the child to name a number and pop the correct finger up. Then challenge the child to tell you the number on the finger that you have chosen to put up. Move the fingers of the glove as you enjoy familiar counting rhymes

together, such as 'Five Currant Buns' (see page 41) or 'Five Fat Sausages Sizzling in the Pan' (Traditional).

Use the glove to develop a game, asking questions such as, 'How many cuddles shall we give Teddy?' or 'How many kisses shall we pop on to his nose?'. Invite the child to wear the glove and to give you tasks to do too.

Special support
This activity is gentle and has a narrow focus of attention for a child who is in bed. Keep the activities short and finish before the child tires or loses interest.

Extension
Add the numerals 6 to 10 on to a second pair of gloves. Move the fingers as you sing the nursery rhyme 'One, Two, Three, Four, Five, Once I Caught a Fish Alive' (Traditional).

LINKS WITH HOME
The parents or carers can play with the glove, holding up a number finger and challenging their child to 'clap *three* times', 'find *two* spoons' and so on.

Bandages

Group size
Two children at a time.

What you need
A selection of large teddies or soft toys; different lengths of crêpe bandage, some of them very long and some very short.

What to do
Introduce the children to the teddies and show them how they can use the bandages, tucking in the ends to keep them in place. Tell the children that Teddy has fallen off a wall and hurt his leg. Can the children find a good bandage that will wrap up Teddy's leg comfortably? Talk about why we use bandages to keep parts of the body from swelling or moving when they are injured.

Continue the game with your stories, bringing in other of Teddy's friends and describing their injuries. Encourage the children to use describing words when looking for the next bandage, for example, 'We need a *longer* one for the tummy, this one is *too short*', 'We need a *shorter* one for the thumb, this one is *too long*' and so on. You will end up with a whole hospital ward of bandaged toys, so this activity can lead easily into hospital play!

Special support
For children who are often cared for by doctors and others, this 'caring' activity will make a refreshing change. It can also be used as a starting-point for talking about medical treatment.

Extension
Lead into some very simple first-aid facts at a level of understanding to suit the children.

LEARNING OBJECTIVE FOR ALL THE CHILDREN
● to use language such as 'longer' and 'shorter', to compare two lengths.

INDIVIDUAL LEARNING TARGET
● to enjoy role-playing the 'carer' instead of the 'cared for'.

LINKS WITH HOME
Invite the children to bring in a favourite teddy from home. Ask parents and carers to look for other opportunities to use the words 'longer' and 'shorter' – for example, when talking about hair-styles.

Magnetic number gym

Group size
One poorly child.

What you need
A magnet board (about A4 size for easy handling); several sets of plastic magnetic numerals, 1 to 5.

What to do
Here are some ideas for playing with magnetic numerals:

- Put up the numbers in order, 1 to 5. Count out loud as you do so and encourage the child to count with you. Repeat, but ask the child to do the counting.
- Place the numbers in order and challenge the child to 'point to number 2' and so on. Place the numbers in random order and challenge the child again.
- Place all the numbers in a pot. Ask the child to find a number 3 and so on.
- Place the numbers in a row but with one number missing. Ask the child to put the missing number in place.
- Ask the child to find all the number 1s (and so on) and put them on the board.
- Make a string of numbers on the board. Ask the child to copy it with a second string of numbers just beneath.
- Ask the child to find the number which says how old they are.
- Put up the numbers in reverse order and practise saying them backwards.

Special support
Choose activities which suit the stage, ability and general state of health of the child you are playing with.

Extension
Play a memory game. Give the child a string of three or four numbers and ask them to find the corresponding plastic numbers and put these up on the board in the right order.

Paper clowns

Group size
One child at a time, perhaps a poorly child in bed.

What you need
A long strip of paper (made out of 10 sheets of A4 paper placed side to side and stuck with sticky tape, or the equivalent length cut from a paper roll); washable felt-tipped pens; black felt-tipped pen; tray to work on if the child is in bed; copy of the photocopiable sheet on page 87; scissors; small circular coloured stickers (approximately 5mm in diameter).

What to do
Fold your strip of paper zigzag style with the first fold on the right-hand side (see diagram, right).

Cut out the template from the photocopiable sheet and use it to draw around. Help the child to cut around the outline. Open up the zigzag to find all the clowns. Now enjoy colouring these in. Look for patterns and try to make each clown different or all the clowns the same.

Use a black felt-tipped pen to number the clowns 1 to 10 on their tummies. Pretend that the stickers are pompoms. Encourage the child to stick one on the '1' clown, two on the '2' clown and so on. Hang the clowns up where they can be admired and counted. Touch each one in order and ask the child to call out the correct number.

Special support
These clowns can be hung above a hospital bed and admired by visitors.

Extension
You can enjoy this activity in a group too. See what other 'paper-doll chains' you can invent together.

LEARNING OBJECTIVE FOR ALL THE CHILDREN
● to talk about, recognize and re-create simple patterns.

INDIVIDUAL LEARNING TARGET
● to enjoy creating a decoration at home or in hospital.

LEARNING OBJECTIVE FOR ALL THE CHILDREN
● to say and use number names in order in familiar contexts.

INDIVIDUAL LEARNING TARGET
● to teach a number rhyme to a carer.

Five little pixies

Group size
One child who is feeling quiet or unwell.

What you need
A willing helper or visitor to the poorly child; small circular stickers (about 1cm in diameter); pen.

What to do
Familiarize yourself with this rhyme:

> Five little pixies all in a row,
> Jumping high and creeping low,
> See them wiggle, see them fly,
> Stand up straight, then wave goodbye!
>
> *Hannah Mortimer*

Hold your fingers apart for the first line; shoot them high then crawl them along low for the second line; wiggle and then flap them for the third; stiffen them then bend them to wave goodbye for the last line! Now teach the rhyme to the child.

As a variation, give each finger a sticker with a number from 1 to 5, in order. Ask 'pixie number one' to wave goodbye. Then ask for 'pixie

number three' to fly high. Next, say, 'Can "pixie number two" creep along the bedclothes?', and so on.

When the child is confident with the words, suggest that they teach it to their next visitor. Do they think that they can remember it? Have a practice. Invite the next visiting friend, relative or nurse to learn a new rhyme from the patient!

Special support
When the child returns to the group, ask them to teach the finger rhyme to the other children.

Extension
Think of other action rhymes on fingers and toes that can be joined in , such as 'This Little Piggy Went to Market' (Traditional).

LINKS WITH HOME
Lend parents and carers a book of action rhymes and songs so that they can sing them to their child when they are away from the group or ill in bed.

LEARNING OBJECTIVE FOR ALL THE CHILDREN
● to begin to use the vocabulary involved in adding and subtracting.

INDIVIDUAL LEARNING TARGET
● to feel relaxed and comfortable while learning.

Then there were none

Group size
Two to four children.

What you need
A farm layout with fields and yards; toy farm animals; toy farmer.

What to do
Set up the farm together. Put the buildings in place and put up any fences. Now invite the children to put all the pigs in one field, all the cows in another, all the sheep in a third and all the ducks in the pond (and so on if you have more space!). Count them out together.

Now make the farmer come along and say, 'Farmer Jones wants three pigs to go to bed now. Can you take away three pigs from the field?'. Invite one child to do this, and ask the other children to count the remaining pigs all together. Make a similar request for the sheep, ducks and cows. Each time, help a child to take away the right number of animals and put them in the sheds, and assist the other children with counting out how many are left in the field. Continue until you can say, 'And then there was none'.

Special support
When children are convalescing or recovering from treatment, they might welcome the chance to play quietly with floor or table-top toys. Do not be surprised if the child's play is more repetitive or at a younger level than usual.

Extension
Write down what you have done as a sum, explaining to the children what you are writing, for example, 6 pigs – 2 pigs = 4 pigs; 4 pigs – 4 pigs = 0 pigs.

LINKS WITH HOME
Suggest a simple counting game that parents and carers can play at mealtimes with their children: 'How many fishfingers do you have on your plate? Can you eat up one? How many are left?'.

KNOWLEDGE AND UNDERSTANDING OF THE WORLD

Help the children to find out more about the world of health and medicine and about their bodies, with these ideas for feeling comfortable and relaxed when receiving treatment at home or in hospital.

LEARNING OBJECTIVES FOR ALL THE CHILDREN
● to ask questions about why things happen and how things work
● to find out about medicines.

INDIVIDUAL LEARNING TARGET
● to understand more about their own medication.

LINKS WITH HOME
Work out your policy for giving medicines in the group (see page 10) and share this with parents and carers.

All about medicines

Group size
Six to 20 children.

What you need
General knowledge about medicines and safety (see Chapter 1); empty medicine and pill bottles; inhaler (optional).

What to do
Gather the children together and show them the empty containers. Have any of the children ever had to take medicine? Why do people take medicine? Explain that medicines can sometimes help to make people better, and are sometimes taken to make people *feel* better when they are unwell, perhaps by stopping the pain.

Tell the children that although medicines can help you get better, they can also harm you if you take too many or somebody else's. Explain the safety rules, showing your empty containers as examples of bottles that the children should never play with.

The key discussion points are:
● Never play with medicines.
● Tell your parents or carers if you find any medicines lying around. Do not touch them.
● Never take medicines that belong to someone else.
● Always do what the doctor has told you about your medicine.
● Most medicines should be given to you by a grown-up (though some young children learn to use inhalers on their own).

End the activity by singing the song 'Miss Polly Had a Dolly' (see page 46) and explaining what a prescription is.

Special support
Some children might welcome the chance to talk to other children about their own medicines. Others might prefer to talk to you individually.

Extension
Invite the school doctor or nurse to visit you to talk simply about the different kinds of medicines.

Ambulance!

Group size
All the children.

What you need
A visit from the local ambulance service; extra adult helpers.

What to do
Set up this activity well ahead. Contact your local ambulance service to see whether they will arrange educational visits, perhaps by a paramedic. Alternatively, contact the St John Ambulance Brigade for your area (Tel: 0870-235 5231 or visit their website at www.sja.org.uk). If there is a child who has had particular experiences with ambulances, you might mention this in general terms to explain why you are so keen for the visit. Say that the children would be interested in seeing some of the equipment and hearing the siren, perhaps even trying lying on the stretcher. Explain that the visit will need to be short to hold their interest. (You will also be told that the visit will have to be cut short if the crew is called away suddenly.)

On the day of the visit, try to spend five minutes with the ambulance crew before the children can come out so that you will be ready to explain to them very simply what everything is for. Bring the children out and encourage them to ask questions and try things out where safe to do so.

Special support
If possible, save the siren till last and take the more timid children inside to listen to it!

Extension
Follow up with small-world play or imaginative play around the theme of ambulances.

LEARNING OBJECTIVE FOR ALL THE CHILDREN
● to find out about and identify some features of objects and events they observe.

INDIVIDUAL LEARNING TARGET
● to make sense of any experiences they might have had involving ambulances.

LINKS WITH HOME
If a child has been worried about ambulances, make sure that a parent or carer stays close to them. Explain that children can always have somebody with them if they travel in an ambulance. Let the children take home a copy of the photocopiable sheet on page 88 to colour in and to talk about.

Tara's new hat

Group size
Four to six children.

What you need
A copy of the story on the photocopiable sheet on page 89; easels; paper; paintbrushes; paints.

What to do
Gather the children around you. Read through the story on the photocopiable sheet, then talk about it together. Explain that because of her illness, Tara needed a very strong medicine. Tell the children that medicines do not usually make your hair fall out, but some medicines have to be very strong in order to fight big illnesses.

Now ask the children to think about Tara's hat. It must have been a wonderful hat! Talk about what the hat might have looked like and discuss the colours and the shapes. Invite each child to paint a picture of Tara in her new hat. Stay close to talk with the children as they work, picking up any more questions and comments that they want to make.

Special support
You might be able to use this story sensitively if there is a child undergoing chemotherapy treatment. You can also use this story individually in order to make their experiences seem more 'normal' and to provide a starting-point for asking questions or sharing feelings.

Extension
Try creating a new hat for Tara out of coloured card, crêpe paper and shiny paper. Let the children try the hat on and suggest that they admire the effect in front of a mirror.

LEARNING OBJECTIVE FOR ALL THE CHILDREN
● to ask questions about why things happen.

INDIVIDUAL LEARNING TARGET
● to be able to make sense of what they are experiencing following chemotherapy.

LINKS WITH HOME
Talk with the parents or carers of a child affected before doing this activity. Share your story and make sure that you have a full understanding of the particular child's illness before including them in this activity, as not all chemotherapy leads to loss of hair, for example.

LEARNING OBJECTIVE FOR ALL THE CHILDREN
● to select appropriate resources for a toy project in the local surgery.

INDIVIDUAL LEARNING TARGET
● to have entertaining toys and activities to play with when visiting the surgery.

Going to the doctor's

Group size
All the children.

What you need
A large toy chest or plastic box; selection of toys.

What to do
In this activity, you will design and put together a toy chest for your local GP's surgery. Contact the local practice nurses and explore this suggestion. They might be very pleased to make a link with your setting, in which you would bring their waiting-room toys up to date.

Gather the children together and have a discussion about going to the doctor's. Talk about the reception area, the waiting-room and going in to see the doctor. What do the children do while they are waiting?

Talk about the toys and what the children played with while waiting for the doctor. Quite often, the toys will have been few and incomplete. Share ideas of toys which would be good to play with in a waiting-room. Talk about how they need to be safe for little children, yet interesting for older ones, but also how they should not take too long to play with. Are lots of small parts (as in a jigsaw puzzle) a good idea? Think of ideas for toys, books and activities, and put them together in a toy chest or plastic box for your local surgery.

Special support
If a child has to make frequent visits to the surgery, ask them and their parents or carers to be your 'link'. Suggest that they let you know how the toys are now being enjoyed and played with, and which need replacing.

Extension
Ask the children to invent a good toy for a waiting-room and draw it.

LINKS WITH HOME
Put together a letter that you can send to parents and carers, full of the children's ideas. Ask for used but unbroken toys to build up a special box to give to the surgery.

LEARNING OBJECTIVE FOR ALL THE CHILDREN
● to find out and observe the uses of medical technology.

INDIVIDUAL LEARNING TARGET
● to make sense of some of their experiences in hospital.

Children's ward

Group size
Six to eight children.

What you need
A copy of the photocopiable sheet on page 90 for each child; coloured pens or crayons; toy medical kits; dressing-up clothes; 'hospital corner' in your playroom; if available, a copy of *Hospital* by Althea (Happy Cat Books).

What to do
Sit down together in your story corner and share your picture book about hospitals. Has anyone ever been to hospital? Some of the children might have visited a relative or friend, others might have been there for treatment. Most will have seen hospitals on television. Share your experiences and talk about some of the reasons people go to hospital and some of the treatments that they have. Tell the group that not everyone sleeps there. Explain that there is a lot of very special equipment, and talk about the X-ray machines, scanners and the special apparatus to help people breathe and to help their blood work.

Give each child a copy of the photocopiable sheet and talk about what is happening in the children's ward. Encourage each child to colour over their picture, and talk together about hospitals as they work.

Special support
Photocopy the sheet on to A3 paper for younger children to colour over. Stay close to any child who has been hospitalized recently so that you can talk with them about their own experiences if they would like to.

Extension
Organize a hospital role-play. Provide bits and pieces that the children can imagine as special hospital equipment. Ask the children what the equipment is for and how it helps the patient.

LINKS WITH HOME
Build up a library of useful pamphlets and picture books about medical conditions. Lend *Hospital* to the parents or carers of a child who is due for a visit.

LEARNING OBJECTIVE FOR ALL THE CHILDREN
● to talk about features of their environment that they like and dislike.

INDIVIDUAL LEARNING TARGET
● to visualize a special place that makes them feel calm and relaxed.

My special place

Group size
Three or four children.

What you need
A script for a simple visualization exercise (you may adapt the idea below) or take an idea from, for example, *More Quality Circle Time, Volume 2* by Jenny Mosley (LDA).

What to do
Gather the children together, lying back comfortably on cushions. Suggest that you rest and relax for a few moments. Discuss what to 'relax' means. Suggest that it means keeping still and peaceful. Talk together about places that you love to be in when you want to be peaceful. Suggest to the children (but do not insist) that they close their eyes and take some deep slow breaths with you. Count slowly '1, 2, 3' as you breathe in and '1, 2, 3, 4, 5' as you breathe out more slowly. Then read your 'visualization' script to the children, for example:

> Imagine that you are in a beautiful room. There are long curtains and a thick carpet. Feel the carpet between your toes as you wiggle them. On the floor are some beautiful cushions. You lie down on the cushions and stretch out. Can you stretch out your legs? Point your toes out, now relax and make your legs go still and floppy. Can you stretch out your arms? Now let them flop back on to the cushions. Take a big yawn. Now relax. Imagine your own special room and look around it, admiring all your favourite things. Feel the happiness pouring through you as you rest.

Help the children to liven up again gradually by saying, for example, 'Now it's time for us to have drinks, so we are going to open our eyes, have one more stretch and get up slowly.'

Special support
Simple visualization exercises are helpful for children who need to relax and to control their discomfort or pain. By practising imagining their favourite place, a child can gradually just think about it when they need to relax.

Extension
Draw a beautiful picture of a favourite place.

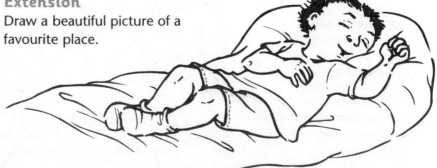

LINKS WITH HOME
If this approach is effective for a child who is in discomfort, share it with the parents or carers and give them a possible script.

LEARNING OBJECTIVE FOR ALL THE CHILDREN
● to ask questions about why things happen and how infections can be spread.

INDIVIDUAL LEARNING TARGET
● to feel confident when talking about illnesses.

Coughs and sneezes

Group size
Six to 20 children.

What you need
A box of tissues; waste-paper bucket.

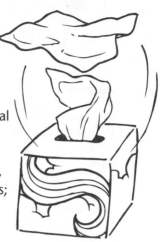

What to do
Gather the children in a circle for the traditional nursery rhyme:

> Ring-o-Ring-o-Roses,
> A pocket full of posies;
> Atishoo, atishoo,
> We all fall down.

Another favourite action rhyme with sneezing in is 'Mousie' in *Round and Round the Garden* (Oxford University Press).

Spend a few moments talking about coughs and sneezes. They are sometimes signs that somebody has a cold. Introduce the word 'germ' and explain that when people catch colds it is because they have caught cold germs from someone else. Cold germs give you blocked noses and this sometimes makes you sneeze. But when you sneeze, more germs get blown into the air! That is why people 'catch' colds from one another.

Invite the children to think about how we can stop colds from being passed on. Talk about blowing noses and show the children your tissues and the waste-paper bucket. Say that you are going to be looking for lots of used tissues in that bucket to see whether the children are really thinking about keeping their colds to themselves. Place the bucket and tissues handy and dispose of the contents safely after each session.

Special support
Some children sneeze because of hay fever. If this is the case in your setting, you can talk about hay fever too, explaining that it's not contagious, but suggesting that it is still a good idea to use the tissues and bucket.

Extension
Talk together about all the reasons why children might need to stay at home when they are feeling unwell.

LINKS WITH HOME
Encourage parents and carers to help their children learn to blow their noses independently. Warn the carers of children with chronic medical conditions if there are germs around.

LEARNING OBJECTIVE FOR ALL THE CHILDREN
● to ask questions about how bodies work.

INDIVIDUAL LEARNING TARGET
● to understand more about their body.

My body

Group size
Two to six children at a time (an even number).

What you need
A roll of paper; washable thick felt-tipped pens; picture of the human body, including bones and muscles (such as the *Human Anatomy Flip Chart*, available from NES Arnold).

What to do
Gather the children around you and show them your pictures of the human body. Ask them what they think they have got inside them. At this early stage, you may find that they understand that they have bones, blood and perhaps a tummy and heart inside. Talk in very simple terms about how different parts of the body help you move, breathe, see, smell and hear.

Now help the children to choose a partner to work with. Roll out strips of paper, a bit longer than the children, on to a smooth floor. Show the children how to lie flat and still while their partners draw around them. Then ask the pairs to swap roles.

Now support the children as they work on the floor filling in as many body parts as they know about (inside and out) – a simple skeleton perhaps, a tummy and a heart, the nose, ears, mouth and eyes. Help the children to name these as they work and talk about how they help us. Hang the pictures up along a wall so that you can share them and talk about them later.

Special support
Children with particular medical conditions, such as kidney disease, are likely to know more about the organ affected than the other children. This, of course, may not mean that they understand about other body parts too.

Extension
Invite the children to make a lift-the-flap book with a child on the flap and a simple skeleton underneath.

LINKS WITH HOME
Ask parents and carers to help by asking their children to point to simple body parts.

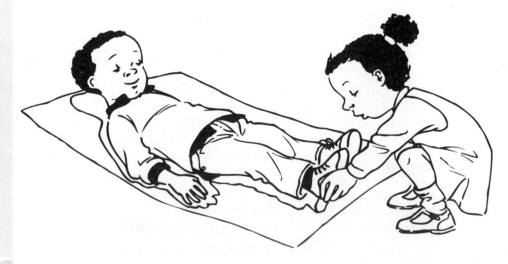

PHYSICAL DEVELOPMENT

Children who are convalescing sometimes need to do special exercises, eat special foods or learn to relax in order to control their discomfort. The ideas in this chapter show how you can build these requirements into your group activities.

LEARNING OBJECTIVE FOR ALL THE CHILDREN

● to recognize the changes that happen to their bodies when they are active.

INDIVIDUAL LEARNING TARGET

● to reduce exercise-induced asthma and learn to pace themselves.

LINKS WITH HOME

If a child has exercise-induced asthma, ask the parents or carers whether they should have a dose of reliever medication before they do exercise.

Warming up

Group size
All the children.

What you need
A large floor space and a full-length mirror, if available; adult helper; soft shoes or plimsolls for the children (or they could be bare feet).

What to do
This is a warm-up activity to do before a physical education class. Move into your large area and ask each child to find a space to themselves. Stand facing all the children so that you can model the following exercises for them:

● Reach up high, stretch your fingers and rise on to your toes. Feel the stretch! Now relax and shake yourselves. Repeat this three times.
● Reach down low and touch your toes. Try to keep your legs straight! Now relax and shake yourselves. Repeat three times.
● Now walk slowly on the spot and swing your arms. Move more quickly, gathering speed until you are really running on the spot, then stop. Relax and rest.
● Repeat the running on the spot three times and then rest.
    The whole set of exercises should last about five minutes.
    Start to talk about the changes in your bodies. Have a look in the mirror. What do the children notice? Talk about how your heart beats faster, your breathing speeds up and your face goes red. Watch the signs change as your body slows down again.

Special support
Your aim is to help the child with asthma to recognize changes in their body so that they can learn to pace themselves. It is usually good for them to take part in exercise so long as it is paced. Talk to the carers first so that you know how much exercise the child can tolerate. If breathing becomes laboured, stop and sit them down, breathing slowly and deeply with them.

Extension
Talk simply about how the heart, breathing and blood work together in our bodies.

LEARNING OBJECTIVE FOR ALL THE CHILDREN
● to recognize the changes that happen to their bodies when they are calm.

INDIVIDUAL LEARNING TARGET
● to be able to relax somewhere calm when they need to.

The resting rug

Group size
Any child who needs to rest after or during exercise.

What you need
A soft rug or similar; attractive floor cushions; if outdoors, a parasol to provide shade.

What to do
Set up this activity when you are doing energetic exercise in a hall or outdoor area. Start by warming everyone up (see 'Warming up' on page 69). Then move on to your physical-activity session.

Every now and again, pause the activity and invite children who feel tired to put up their hands. Encourage two or three children at a time to take a rest on the resting rug. Talk to all the children about how their bodies change with exercise and then with rest. When these children have rested, allow another group of children to have a turn on the rug.

If possible, look for ways of keeping the children on the rug still involved. Ideas include:
● If the children are making different shapes with their bodies, those on the rug can help you judge the spikiest, the roundest and so on.
● If the children are playing a 'Pirates' game on the apparatus, those on the rug can spot whether someone steps off into the 'sea'.
● A resting child could help by blowing a whistle to start or stop an activity.

Special support
If there is a child who is not able to do physical exercise, this rug will provide them with a resting area. In this way, a child who is convalescing or unwell can still watch what is happening and feel included, especially as they will be sharing the rug with others.

Extension
Encourage the children to think about why their hearts pump less when they are resting.

LINKS WITH HOME
Encourage parents and carers to write you a note when their children cannot do physical exercise. If any carer is helping you, perhaps they could sit with these children on the resting rug and talk about what is happening.

PHYSICAL DEVELOPMENT • PHYSICAL DEVELOPMENT • PHYSICAL DEVELOPMENT

LEARNING OBJECTIVE FOR ALL THE CHILDREN
● to recognize the importance of staying healthy and those things which contribute to this.

INDIVIDUAL LEARNING TARGET
● to talk about their allergies and their diet.

Food fun

Group size
All the children.

What you need
Natural and fresh foods from many cultures (wholemeal bread and butter, unprocessed cheese, natural yoghurt with fruit purée, fresh fruit, raw vegetables, couscous, home-made savoury rice and so on); plates; spoons; kitchen knife (adult use); cling film; packaging from highly-processed foods such as fizzy drinks, dry noodles, lollipops and biscuits.

What to do
First, check for any dietary requirements or food allergies. Prepare the food in advance, cutting it into bite-size portions or arranging it in serving bowls and covering.

Gather the children together. Talk about what they like to eat, then what foods they think are really good for them. Talk about fruit and vegetables for staying healthy; milk, cheese and yoghurts for helping to grow strong, and so on. The children are bound to mention sweets, crisps, biscuits as being their favourite foods. Ask them, 'Are the foods that you like always good for you?'. Let the children work this out with their own ideas. Explain that sometimes children have to stop eating certain food because it is bad for them. Introduce the word 'allergic'. Then suggest that the children taste some foods that are really good for them and see if they also taste good.

Enjoy your tasting session together.

Special support
Children who are allergic to certain food might welcome the chance to talk about this with the other children.

Extension
Encourage the children to sort pictures of healthy food from pictures of food which is not so healthy.

LINKS WITH HOME
Send home a list of really healthy foods that a child enjoyed at your tasting session.

LEARNING OBJECTIVE FOR ALL THE CHILDREN
● to move fingers with control and co-ordination.

INDIVIDUAL LEARNING TARGET
● to enjoy a simple physical exercise even if you are feeling tired or weak.

Slowly, slowly

Group size
12 to 20 children.

What you need
A copy of the rhyme on the photocopiable sheet on page 91 for each child to take home; wide space for running in.

What to do
Gather in a circle, sitting on the floor. Ask the children to copy whatever you do. Start by clapping your hands very slowly in a steady rhythm. Then pause and wait for the children to stop too. Now clap your hands very quickly, again in a steady rhythm. Stop and praise the children for trying. Now try the same rhythms, but this time tapping the palm of your hand with two fingers used together as a beater.

Teach the children the rhyme on the photocopiable sheet. Encourage them to tap their palms as you say the first verse slowly and steadily and the second quickly, ending with a final tap for 'flash!'.

Finish the activity by standing up and first plodding, then scampering around the space, to the rhythm of the words. On the word 'flash!', encourage all the children to crouch down low.

LINKS WITH HOME
Send a copy of the rhyme home for the children to enjoy with their parents or carers. Make sure that any child who is unwell receives a copy too.

Special support
This is a gentle activity for a carer and child to do together when sitting quietly or when the child is in bed. The carer should say the rhyme as they tap the child's palm, or hold out their palm for them to tap.

Extension
Use some fast and slow drumbeats for the children to listen and respond to by plodding or scampering around.

LEARNING OBJECTIVE FOR ALL THE CHILDREN
● to recognize changes in their bodies when active.

INDIVIDUAL LEARNING TARGET
● to use big breaths for staying calm.

Big breaths

Group size
One child at a time.

What you need
Familiarize yourself with the rhyme below.

What to do
This activity is to help a child breathe fully and deeply. Perhaps they are calming down after physical exercise or shock, perhaps they are recovering from an asthma attack, or perhaps they are learning to breathe through their pain.

First, help the child to place their hands lightly on their lower chest so that they can feel it move, pushing their hands outwards and upwards as they breathe in and out. Ask them to copy you as you show them how to breathe calmly. It will take a little time, so continue your own regular pattern of breaths until the child matches yours.

Now chant the rhyme below softly as the child breathes in slowly for the first line and out for the second, and so on. Emphasize the numbers in the rhyme and say the words more softly. In time, you can replace the rhyme with the words 'one – two' (slow count for breathing in) and 'three – four – five – six – seven' (slightly longer breathing out).

> One little alligator, two little alligators,
> Three four five six seven little alligators,
> Resting in the river where nobody goes,
> Waiting for the moment when they see your toes!
> One little alligator, two little alligators,
> Three four five six seven little alligators,
> Snoozing in the river in the midday sun,
> Best not wake them, anyone!
>
> *Hannah Mortimer*

Special support
This simple breathing exercise is also fun to do. Use it when a child needs to calm themselves or control their own discomfort or pain. Children with asthma often find it easier to breathe slowly sitting up or leaning slightly forwards.

Extension
Use this breathing exercise before a visualization story (see page 66).

LINKS WITH HOME
If this rhyme is effective, share it with parents and carers to use at times of upset at home or in hospital.

LEARNING OBJECTIVE FOR ALL THE CHILDREN
● to blow with control.

INDIVIDUAL LEARNING TARGET
● to develop breath control.

Caterpillar race

Group size
Three or four children at a time.

What you need
Cotton-wool balls; coloured washable inks; paintbrushes; big drinking straws; smooth and clean floor surface.

What to do
Give each child a cotton-wool ball and show how it can be gently unwound into a strip of cotton wool. Explain that they are going to make a caterpillar shape by rolling the strip gently on a table surface to make it roughly cylindrical.

Now show each child how they can dab their 'caterpillar' with coloured inks to decorate it. Make a few spares in case of 'accidents'. Place the caterpillars somewhere to dry. When they are dry, show the children how they can use the straws to blow them along the floor. See how quickly they can cross the floor or 'crawl' all around the room! Can they move in a straight line? Can they go round in circles? Can they all get together? Can they all find a space of their own? Encourage the children to talk about what they are doing and how it makes them feel.

LINKS WITH HOME
Suggest to parents and carers that they play some simple blowing games with their children, using straws and feathers or ping-pong balls.

Special support
This is a useful activity for building up breath control for children who might be short of breath or learning how to breathe correctly. If a child feels dizzy, it will be because they are hyperventilating or breathing out too hard. Help them to stop and sit with their head lowered.

Extension
Invite the children to make a simple obstacle course for their caterpillars.

LEARNING OBJECTIVE FOR ALL THE CHILDREN

● to recognize changes in their bodies when they relax.

INDIVIDUAL LEARNING TARGET

● to learn to relax.

LINKS WITH HOME
This might be a helpful rhyme to share with the parents or carers of a child with chronic pain or discomfort. It can also be tried to help any child relax at bedtime!

Peace!

Group size
One or two children at a time.

What you need
Space with cushions and a rug to relax.

What to do
Familiarize yourself with the rhyme below. When a child needs to relax, encourage them to lie back and make themselves comfortable.

Say the rhyme. As you say the second line, help the child to tighten each foot then let it relax and fall back gently. For the second line, tighten the knees and then relax. Gradually work up from toes to eyes, tightening and then relaxing each part of the body. Take the rhyme very slowly so that, by the end of it, the child should feel relaxed all over.

> Here comes peace!
> Here we go! It's reached my toe…
> Oh me! It's reached my knee…
> Oh my! It's reached my thigh…
> That's funny! It's reached my tummy…
> Have a rest! It's reached my chest…
> Staying calm, it's reached my arm…
> Go to bed, it's reached my head…
> Close my eyes, pretend to sleep…
> PEACE… PEACE…

When you have finished relaxing, start moving again slowly and gently, rising slowly to your feet and stretching.

Special support
In time, children can learn the relaxation routine if you chant the words slowly. They can also learn to begin to relax when you reassure them and softly say, 'Peace'.

Extension
As the children learn the rhyme, encourage them to talk about how each part of their bodies feels when it is tight and then when it is relaxed.

PHYSICAL DEVELOPMENT • PHYSICAL DEVELOPMENT

LEARNING OBJECTIVE FOR ALL THE CHILDREN
● to move with control and co-ordination.

INDIVIDUAL LEARNING TARGET
● to carry out simple stretching exercises for stiffened limbs.

LINKS WITH HOME
If a child has had recent surgery, ask the parents or carers what movements you should be encouraging or preventing. Encourage all the parents to be active with their children, such as by playing football or taking walks together.

Bend and stretch

Group size
Six to ten children.

What you need
An open space to move in; CD player or tape recorder and some rhythmical music.

What to do
Pretend that this is a 'keep fit' class. The children should watch you carefully and try to copy everything that you do. Stand in front of them and begin to do the following exercises:
● Move your neck slowly to one side and then to the other.
● Move your neck to look slowly down at your feet then up in the air.
● Move your head slowly in a circular movement in both directions.
● Stretch your hands up in the air with your fingers reaching up, then lower them to your side.
● Keep your hands straight and stretch them round to one side at tummy level, reaching behind you. Repeat the other side.
● Keep your arms straight and reach down to your toes, moving them in a gentle circle to the sides clockwise, then straighten up as you stretch them high above your head. Repeat for the other direction.

Keep it fun and not too energetic. Practise each exercise five times. Count slowly '1, 2, 3, 4' as you make each movement, counting one number for each bar of the music. The idea is to move and stretch in a controlled way, rather than jerkily and quickly.

Special support
These are gentle exercises for stiffened limbs, but they are fun for everyone. If a child is receiving post-operative physiotherapy, you might be able to build some of their gentle exercises into your 'keep fit' session.

Extension
Continue with other 'keep fit' exercises, adapted to suit the children's ability and concentration.

CREATIVE DEVELOPMENT

Colour, textures and music can all help children to feel good when they are unwell. The following activities show how to develop the children's creative skills while including a child who is poorly at home or in hospital.

LEARNING OBJECTIVE FOR ALL THE CHILDREN
● to explore colour, texture, shape and form in three dimensions.

INDIVIDUAL LEARNING TARGET
● to enjoy a bouquet of flowers from friends in the setting.

A bunch of flowers

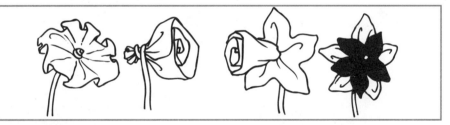

Group size
Three or four children.

What you need
Blu-Tack; sheets of coloured tissue paper; coloured pipe-cleaners; scissors; pot; coloured pens.

What to do
If there is a child who is going into hospital for an operation or who has been ill at home, gather the children together and suggest that you all send the child some home-made flowers and cards. Show the children the tissue paper and admire the different colour combinations as you lay them together. Discuss which colours would look beautiful together to make flowers. Give the children some ideas as to how they can shape and join the tissue petals to the pipe-cleaner stalks (see illustration below).

'Roses' can be made by rolling strips of tissue and then binding them round with one end of the pipe-cleaner. 'Poppies' can be made by cutting discs of tissue and threading the pipe-cleaner through. 'Daisies' can be made by fringing the edges of the petals. Encourage the children to experiment and invent their own flower shapes too. Add little dabs of Blu-Tack to hold petals and stalks in place. Place the flowers gently into a pot. When you have a selection, encourage the children to choose colours as you bind groups of flowers with another pipe-cleaner and wrap them in sheets of tissue paper to look like a bouquet.

Special support
Give each child a copy of the photocopiable sheet on page 92 and encourage them to colour over the flowers. Help them to fold the sheet into two, tell them what the message says, and help them to write their name (scribing for them if necessary).

Extension
Older children can write their own messages in their cards.

LINKS WITH HOME
This also makes a suitable activity for Mother's Day, a family birthday or a special festival.

CREATIVE DEVELOPMENT • CREATIVE DEVELOPMENT •

LEARNING OBJECTIVE FOR ALL THE CHILDREN

● to explore colour and texture in two dimensions.

INDIVIDUAL LEARNING TARGET

● to feel included and special despite being bedridden.

Magic bedspread

Group size
Two or three children at a time.

What you need
An old cot quilt; needle and thread (adult use); fabric remnants; small soft toys and suitable treats; paper; pens; extra adult help.

What to do
In this activity, you all make a special bed cover full of pockets and surprises, suitable for a child who is absent and bedridden. Try to organize some extra adult help for this activity.

Gather the children together and share your idea. Talk about the child who has to stay in bed at the moment and how they are not able to do very much because they are feeling poorly. Suggest that you make a precious bedspread to cover this child's bed in which you can hide all sorts of treats and messages. Will the children help you to do this?

As each child joins you, ask them to choose a snippet of material which can be sewn on to the quilt on three sides as a pocket. Ask the child to choose a little treat which their friend will enjoy (such as a soft toy, a toy bracelet, or a shiny sticker) to go into the pocket. Support them as they write or dictate a message and add their name. Help them to fold the message up small and add it to the pocket.

Continue to make your bedspread over several sessions.

Special support
When children are very unwell, they can only focus their attention on their immediate surroundings and events. This is one idea for 'bringing their world closer' and holding their interest for a short time.

Extension
Older children can help you to design the pockets on the bedspread.

LINKS WITH HOME
Share ideas with the absent child's parents or carers first, to make sure that it will be a suitable gift at this stage of their illness or recovery.

LEARNING OBJECTIVE FOR ALL THE CHILDREN
● to explore colour, texture and shape in two dimensions.

INDIVIDUAL LEARNING TARGET
● to feel happy and included when receiving a gift from their friends because they are unwell.

Scatter cushions

Group size
Two or three children at a time.

What you need
A loosely-stuffed foam cushion with a silky cover; extra foam; remnants of beautiful fabrics in various textures and hues; embroidery thread and needle (adult use); scissors; tailor's chalk.

What to do
In this activity, you can create a luxurious appliqué cushion to send to a child who is ill in bed or convalescing at home.

Enjoy and talk about the textures and colours of the fabric as you choose and cut shapes which will look beautiful together. Encourage each child to select the fabric that they would like, and decide what shape to cut it – you might suggest swirls, dew drops, blobs and stars. Each shape should be roughly 10cm across. Use your tailor's chalk to help the child draw their shape on their chosen fabric. Help them to cut it out and select a little bit of foam.

Decide where the shape is going to go on the cushion and place the foam between the fabric and the cushion. Ask the child to choose a colour of embroidery thread. Stitch the shape simply around its edge to make a padded shape on the cushion. As each child takes a turn, your cushion will fill with padded shapes and swirls.

Special support
The children can also help to make their own cushions for sitting on at circle or story time.

Extension
Older children can select other interesting textures to add to the cushion, such as shiny braid and silken tassels.

LINKS WITH HOME
Children can also make soft foam shapes by cutting two identical pieces of fabric which you can stitch together for them. These make interesting tree decorations at Christmas, or presents for the family.

LEARNING OBJECTIVE FOR ALL THE CHILDREN
● to use their imagination in art and design.

INDIVIDUAL LEARNING TARGET
● to enjoy craft-making on a small scale at home or in hospital.

Lucky bag

Group size
Three or four children at a time.

What you need
Sheets of coloured and shiny paper and card; stapler (adult use); small pencils and rubbers; sheets of tiny stickers; coloured pipe-cleaners; squares of coloured tissue paper; other small-scale craft materials as available; shiny gift bags, about 10cm x 10cm; scissors.

What to do
Work around a table. Suggest that you each make a 'lucky bag' for the children to take home at the end of term. Let each child choose a gift bag to serve as the container.

Show the children your small pencils and rubbers. Help the children to share these out so that each bag has one pencil and one rubber. Now show them the stickers. Explain that there are six (or other choice) stickers for each bag. Work out where the children should cut the sheets of stickers to get the required number to put in their bags.

Now show the tissue paper. Work out how to cut small squares which can be folded into four and added to the bags. Talk about the colours that the children select. Help them to share out the pipe-cleaners.

Finally, choose some coloured paper and shiny card to cut and make into tiny books which you will staple for the children. Work out what size to make these to fit into the bags.

Special support
One of these 'lucky bags' of craft materials can be taken to a child convalescing at home or receiving treatment in hospital.

Extension
Some children might like to make tiny picture books to go into their bags or to send to a friend in hospital.

LINKS WITH HOME
These 'lucky bags' also make useful presents to take home after an end-of-term celebration or party.

LEARNING OBJECTIVE FOR ALL THE CHILDREN
● to express and communicate their ideas using imaginative puppet play.

INDIVIDUAL LEARNING TARGET
● to enjoy a puppet production when convalescing.

Aladdin's cave

Group size
Three to four children.

What you need
A large cardboard box; card; scissors; felt-tipped pens; short lengths of dowelling; shiny paper; foil; glue; sticky tape; torch; picture book of 'Aladdin' (Traditional).

What to do
Start by sharing the picture book of 'Aladdin' together. Talk about the cave full of treasure and what it must have looked like. Suggest that a child who has been absent for a while might enjoy the story too. Ask the children to help you make a puppet theatre to send to the child at home. Ask them, 'Which part of the story was the most interesting to look at?'. The children will probably suggest the cave.

Turn the box on its end and cut out the top half of the base, retaining it for later (see diagram, right). Show the children how to kneel behind the box and move their hands inside the theatre. Next, with the children's help, draw, colour and cut out an Aladdin figure from card. Use sticky tape to

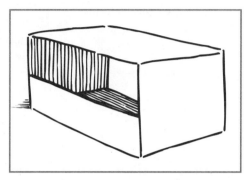

attach him to a length of dowelling to make a stick puppet. Then make stick puppets of the magic lamp and the genie.

Now make the treasure. Encourage the children to select pieces of foil and shiny material to glue to the sides of the 'theatre' and also on to the cardboard that you have cut out of the box which will later serve as the backdrop. When this is dry, hinge it to the back of the theatre with sticky tape.

Act out the scene to the children. Ask one of them to shine a torch to light up the cave.

Special support
With the parents' consent, arrange to take the puppet theatre home to the absent child and show them the play. Leave it for them to play with.

Extension
Let older children make their own stick puppets to act out other stories.

LINKS WITH HOME
Lend the story-book to the parents or carers of the absent child so that they can enjoy the whole story together.

LEARNING OBJECTIVE FOR ALL THE CHILDREN
● to express and communicate their ideas through designing and making hats.

INDIVIDUAL LEARNING TARGET
● to enjoy making and wearing a festive hat.

LINKS WITH HOME
Let the children take their hats home. Ask parents and carers to listen while their children explain how they were made.

Festive hats

Group size
Four to six children at a time.

What you need
The photocopiable sheet on page 93; sheets of shiny and coloured card; scissors; stickers; sticky tape; washable felt-tipped pens; stapler (adult use).

What to do
Make one or two hats in advance to provide ideas for the children. Use the examples on the photocopiable sheet for inspiration.

Ask each child what kind of hat they would like to make. You can probably adapt one of the ideas illustrated to suit their request. Draw the outline of the hat shape on to card for the child to cut out (provide help if necessary). Then encourage them to add stickers or colour to make the detail of their hat.

Finally, bend the hat into shape, adjust the size according to the child's head and staple it into position. Cover the sharp ends of the staples with sticky tape.

Special support
Take a photograph of the children in their hats to send to a child who is away. Making festive hats can also provide fun and entertainment for a child who is unwell at home or in hospital. Try a surgeon's hat or a nurse's hat for a child in a hospital ward.

Extension
Invite the group to make up an imaginative game that involves all your hats, and encourage the children to explore the dressing-up box to complete the effect.

82

LEARNING OBJECTIVES FOR ALL THE CHILDREN
● to explore colour and texture
● to respond in a variety of ways to what they see and feel.

INDIVIDUAL LEARNING TARGET
● to enjoy having their toes decorated and to perform a toe dance from a lying position.

Toe paints

Group size
One bedridden child.

What you need
Non-allergenic nail varnishes in assorted colours; aromatherapy oils; soft towel; some music on a tape or CD; tape recorder or CD player.

What to do
This activity is particularly suitable for a child who can only lie flat. Make sure that the room is warm and fold back the covers of the bed so that their toes are showing. Start with a gentle toe rhyme such as 'This Little Piggy Went to Market' (Traditional), touching and wiggling each toe in turn. If the child enjoys it and the feet are not too sensitive, try a gentle massage with the oils. Some children find this wonderfully relaxing. Dry the feet gently with a soft towel. Now that the toes are looking and smelling so clean and fresh, suggest that you paint some colours on the

nails, imagining, for example, that the first one is a dragon, the second one a piglet, and so on. Build on the child's interests and gradually add colours layer by layer until you have the desired effect. Follow any suggestions that the child is able to make.

At the end, put on some music and invite the child to do a toe dance to the tune. If they are unable to move, then gently touch and move their toes to the music.

Special support
If the child is due for surgery, remember to take in a bottle of nail-varnish remover as you might need to clean the nails before the operation. Check with nursing staff which aromatherapy oils might be appropriate to use.

Extension
Older children can help with the design that you should follow when painting the nails.

LINKS WITH HOME
This activity is a gentle and comforting idea for the parents or carers to do with their child. Check with hospital staff first.

LEARNING OBJECTIVE FOR ALL THE CHILDREN
● to use their imagination in hair and head-dress design.

INDIVIDUAL LEARNING TARGET
● to enjoy being adorned and making faces in a mirror.

LINKS WITH HOME
Parents and carers can play at hairdresser's with their children at home. If they feel brave, they can encourage them to dress their hair! They might need to explain in advance that they will still need to wash it before they next go outdoors!

Shock waves

Group size
One poorly child at home or a group of three to four children.

What you need
Hair gel; temporary (brush-in) hair colour and glitter; scrunchy ribbons; coloured feathers; glittery hairbands; elastic bands; brush; comb; hand-held mirror; large towel.

What to do
Wait until just before the child is due for a hair wash. Suggest that you dress the child's hair up. Would they like it to be spiky and tiger-coloured? Would they like to sparkle and look glamorous? Would they like to look scary?

Start by gently brushing the hair and relaxing the child. Place a towel over their shoulders or pillow. Add gels, colours, glitters and accessories, and follow the child's suggestions. Gels will help you form the hair into spikes or waves. Colours will allow you to give a streaky or patchy effect. Make sure that you have an audience to applaud the changes.

Talk about what the child looks like and encourage them to make expressions with their faces to go with their new hair! You might try face-paints as well if the child's skin is not too sensitive.

Special support
This activity provides a gentle distraction for a child who is unwell or in bed. Take a photograph of the finished hair-styles to send to the group.

Extension
This makes a useful activity to involve an older sibling. Show them how to be gentle when dressing their brother or sister's hair.

Individual health care plan   CONFIDENTIAL

Name:	**Date of birth:**

People contributing to this plan:

Date of plan:	**Medical condition:**

Child's personal symptoms:

Daily care requirements:

What constitutes an emergency for the child?

What action should be taken in an emergency?

Any follow-up care:

Emergency contacts:

1. **Name:**	**Relationship:**
Phone nos: home:	work:
2. **Name:**	**Relationship:**
Phone nos: home:	work:
Clinic/hospital contact: Name:	**Phone no:**
GP: Name:	**Phone no:**

Next review date with parents/carers:

Holding hands

Here is the song we learned to sing today. Try singing it together as you walk home, to the tune of 'Girls and Boys Come Out to Play'.

Mums and children are holding hands
Holding hands as they walk along
Safe from traffic, they're holding hands
Crossing the road together.

Dads and children are holding hands
Holding hands as they walk along
Safe from traffic, they're holding hands
Crossing the road together.

Brothers and sisters are holding hands
Holding hands as they walk along
Safe from traffic, they're holding hands
Crossing the road together.

Hannah Mortimer

Paper clowns

Ambulance!

Parents and carers: talk about this ambulance with your child as you colour it in together.

AMBULANCE

Tara's new hat

Tara wasn't feeling well. For a long time, no one was sure what was wrong. She was feeling very tired and groggy and didn't feel much like eating her favourite dinners. Every time she went outside to play, she would end up crying and coming in again, too tired to have any fun. Her friends couldn't understand why Tara did not want to play with them any more.

Then one day her mum noticed that she was covered with bruises. 'Who has been hurting you?' she asked. Tara hung her head. She knew that nobody had hurt her and she hadn't even fallen over much lately. But it was true, even the slightest bump or bang and she would notice a big bruise coming up. Tara burst into tears, 'It's no one, it just happens.'

'That's IT!' said Mum, 'I'm taking you straight to the doctor. We're going to get this sorted. Let me give you a big cuddle.' Tara had to go to see the doctor lots of times. The doctor took a tiny bit of blood from her arm to find out what was wrong. It didn't hurt because he used the special cream. In the end, the doctor said that Tara had an illness in her blood which meant that her blood did not work properly and she got tired quickly.

Tara had to go to the hospital to see a special doctor. Everyone at the hospital was very kind and they made sure that Tara's illness did not hurt her. The special doctor explained that Tara's illness was called 'leukaemia'. It needed very strong medicine. Unfortunately, it just might mean that Tara's hair would fall out but it would quickly grow back again.

Mum took Tara to the hairdresser's to have her hair cut very short before she took the medicine. She tried on a stunning new head-dress and she admired herself in the mirror. Over the next few weeks, Tara wore this amazing hat. In fact, some of her hair did fall out and it has now grown back again, but Tara has hardly noticed – she is still wearing her beautiful new hat!

Hannah Mortimer

Children's ward

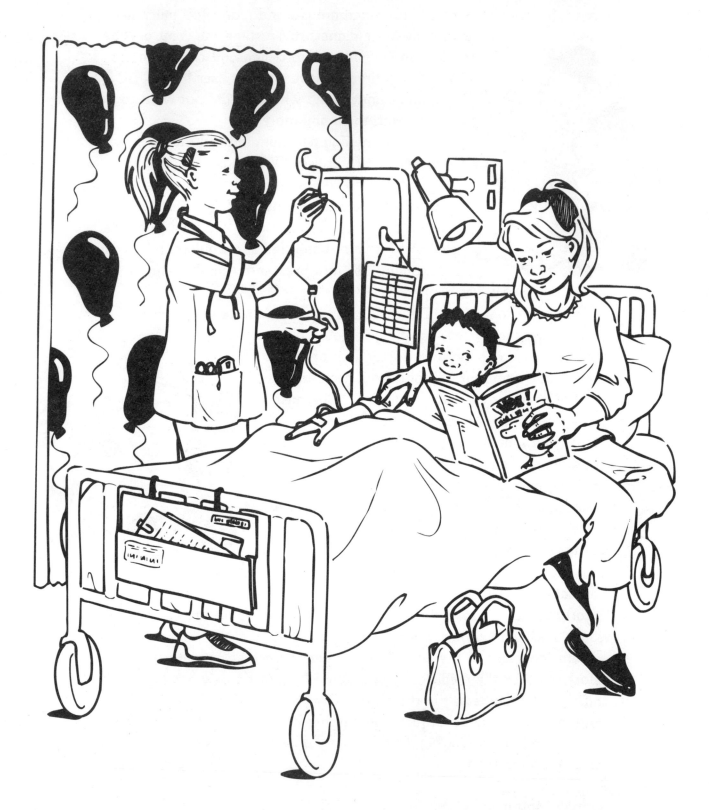

Slowly, slowly

Slowly, slowly, ever so slowly
Goes my tortoise Mister Fred.
Slowly, slowly, ever so slowly
All around the garden shed.

Quickly, quickly, ever so quickly
Goes my little mouse called Dash.
Quickly, quickly, ever so quickly
Here for a moment and gone in a flash!

Hannah Mortimer

Parents and carers:
Help your child to practise
beating the rhythm on the palm
of their hands with two fingers.

A bunch of flowers

Make this card for someone special.

fold

Thinking of you

Coloured by someone who is thinking of you

Festive hats

Who will you pretend to be?

firefighter

surgeon

police officer

soldier

clown

king

RECOMMENDED RESOURCES

ORGANIZATIONS AND SUPPORT GROUPS

● Action for Sick Children, 300 Kingston Road, London SW20 8LX. Tel: 0800-0744519. For advice about supporting children in hospital.

● The Anaphylaxis Campaign, PO Box 275, Farnborough, Hampshire GU14 6SX. Tel: 01252-542029. Produce guidance for carers of pre-school children.

● Association for Children with Life-threatening or Terminal Conditions and their Families (ACT), Orchard House, Orchard Lane, Bristol BS1 5DT. Tel: 0117-9221556.

● Barnardo's, Tanners Lane, Barkingside, Ilford, Essex IG6 1QG. Tel: 020-85508822. For helpful leaflets.

● The British Epilepsy Association, New Anstey House, Gate Way Drive, Yeadon, Leeds LS19 7XY. Tel: 0113-2108800.

● British Psychological Society , St Andrew's House, 48 Princess Road East, Leicester, Leicestershire LE1 7DR. Tel: 0116-2549568.

● The *CaF Directory* of specific conditions and rare syndromes in children with their family support networks can be obtained on subscription from Contact a Family, Equity House, 209–211 City Road, London . EC1V 1JN. Tel: 020-76088700.

● The Child Bereavement Trust, Aston House, West Wycombe, High Wycombe, Buckinghamshire HP14 3AG. Tel: 01494-446648. Supply the *When a Child Grieves* video.

● The Child Death Helpline, The Bereavement Services Department, Great Ormond Street Hospital, Great Ormond Street, London WC1N 3JH. Tel: 020-78138551.

● Children with AIDS Charity, 9 Denbigh Street, London SW1V 2HF. Tel: 020-72335966.

● The Compassionate Friends, 53 North Street, Bristol BS3 1EN. Tel: 0117-9665292. Bereaved parents who have lost a child support others.

● The Cystic Fibrosis Trust, 11 London Road, Bromley, Kent BR1 1BY. Tel: 020-84647211.

● Diabetes UK, 10 Queen Anne Street, London W1G 9LH. Tel: 020-73231531.

● Juvenile Diabetes Research Foundation, 25 Gosfield Street, London W1W 6EB. Tel: 020-74363112.

● Leukaemia CARE Society, 2 Shrubbery Avenue, Worcester, Worcestershire WR1 1QH. Tel: 01905-330003.

● Make-A-Wish Foundation, 329–331 London Road, Camberley, Surrey GU15 3HQ. Tel: 01276-24127. Once-in-a-lifetime treats for families of children with life-threatening conditions.

● National Association for the Education of Sick Children (Present), The Satellite School, Regus Hose, Herald Way, Pegasus Business Park, Castle Donington, Derbyshire DE74 2TZ. Tel: 01332-638599.

● The National Asthma Campaign, Providence House, Providence Place, London N1 0NT. Tel: 020-72262260. Publish various helpful documents for schools, including *School Pack* and *Pre-school Guidelines for Developing an Asthma Policy*.

● National Children's Bureau, 8 Wakley Street, London EC1V 7QE. Tel: 020-78436000. For information and training on most aspects of children's welfare and care, and also for their *Highlights* leaflets

produced in conjunction with Barnardo's, such as *Highlight no 181: Young People with Diabetes*.

● The National Meningitis Trust, Fern House, Bath Road, Stroud, Gloucestershire GL5 3TJ. 24-hour support line: 0345-538118, 24-hour information line: 0891-715577. Produce fact sheets and awareness pamphlets.

● Sargent Cancer Care for Children, Griffin House, 161 Hammersmith Road, London W8 8SG. Tel: 020-87522800. Support for families and professionals, information, publications and financial support.

● The Terence Higgins Trust, 52–54 Grays Inn Road, London WC1X 8JU. Tel: 020-72421010. Information and support concerning HIV/AIDS.

● The Theodora Children's Trust, 42 Pentonville Road, London N1 9HF. Tel: 020-77130044. This charity introduced clown doctors to the UK.

BOOKS FOR ADULTS

● *Counselling Children with Chronic Medical Conditions* by Melinda Edwards and Hilton Davis (British Psychological Society Books)

● *Good Grief – Talking and Learning About Loss and Death, Volume 1, Under-11s* by Barbara Ward et al. (Jessica Kingsley Publishers). Designed for use by teachers to help teach about grief and loss among children.

● *Grief in Children – A Handbook for Adults* by Atle Dyregrov (Jessica Kingsley Publishers)

● *Supporting Bereaved and Dying Children and their Parents* by Martin Herbert (British Psychological Society Books)

● *Supporting Pupils with Medical Needs* (DfEE and Department of Health)

● *What Do We Tell the Children? Books to Use with Children Affected by Illness and Bereavement* by Kerstin Phillips (Paediatric AIDS Resource Centre)

● *When Dad Died – Working Through Loss with People Who Have Learning Disabilities or with Children* by Sheila Hollins and Lester Sireling (Saint George's Mental Health Library)

BOOKS FOR CHILDREN ABOUT THEIR OWN MEDICAL CONDITIONS

● The Magination Press specializes in books which help children to deal with personal problems. Send for a catalogue from The Eurospan Group, 3 Henrietta Street, Covent Garden, London WC2E 8LU. Tel: 020-72400856.

● *Lee, the Rabbit With Epilepsy* by Deborah M Moss (Woodbine House)

● *Little Tree* by Joyce C Mills (Magination Press). A story for children with serious medical problems.

● *Asthma* by Althea (Happy Cat Books)

● *Hospital* by Althea (Happy Cat Books)

● *How Your Body Works* by Althea (Happy Cat Books)

● *I Can't Hear Like You* by Althea (Happy Cat Books)

BOOKS FOR SIBLINGS AND FRIENDS ABOUT MEDICAL CONDITIONS

● *Badger's Parting Gifts* by Susan Varley (Picture Lions). A story about bereavement.

● *Granpa* by John Burningham (Jonathan Cape)

● *Sarah and Puffle – A Story for Children About Diabetes* by Linnea Mulder (Magination Press)

● *What About Me? When Brothers and Sisters Get Sick* by Allan Peterkin (Magination Press)

● *When My Little Sister Died* by Sue Cowlishaw (Merlin Publishing)

WEBSITES

● For information on most conditions, their symptoms and their remedies: www.content.health.msn.com

● The British Epilepsy Association: www.epilepsy.org.uk/bea

● The Department for Education and Skills (DfES) (for parent information and for Government circulars and advice including supporting children with medical needs): www.dfes.gov.uk

RESOURCES

● Philip Green Education, from Hope Education, Hyde Buildings, Ashton Road, Hyde, Cheshire SK14 4SH. Tel: 0870-2433400. For colourful poster packs.

● Learning Development Aids, Primary and Special Needs, Duke Street, Wisbech, Cambridgeshire PE13 2AE. Tel: 01945-463441. Supply *More Quality Circle Time, Volume 2* by Jenny Mosley.

● National Association of Toy and Leisure Libraries, 68 Churchway, London NW1 1LT. Tel: 020-73879592. Send sae to find out where the nearest toy library is.

● NES Arnold, Findel Education, Hyde Buildings, Ashton Road, Hyde, Cheshire SK14 4SH. Tel: 01530-418901.

● Quality for Effective Development (QEd), The Rom Building, Eastern Avenue, Lichfield, Staffordshire WS13 6RN. Tel: 01543-416353. Supply *Starting Out* by Hannah Mortimer (a talk-through approach for parents and carers to help their children with medical conditions or special needs to prepare for a new group).

● Step by Step, Lee Fold, Hyde, Cheshire SK14 4LL. Tel: 0845-3001089.

● Barnardo's (see address on page 94). Supply *All About Me* board game.

ORGANIZATIONS THAT PROVIDE TRAINING COURSES

● Children in Scotland, Princes House, 5 Shandwick Place, Edinburgh EH2 4RG. Tel: 0131-2288484. Courses in early years.

● The Council for Awards in Children's Care and Education (CACHE), 8 Chequer Street, St Albans, Herts AL1 3XZ. Tel: 01727-847636.

● National Association for Special Educational Needs (NASEN) , 4–5 Amber Business Village, Amber Close, Amington, Tamworth, Staffordshire B77 4RP. Tel: 01827-311400. For publications and workshops on all aspects of special needs.

● National Early Years Network, 77 Holloway Road, London N7 8JZ. Tel: 020-76079573. For customized in-house training.

● National Portage Association, PO Box 3075, Yeovil, Somerset BA21 3JE. Tel: 01935-471641. For Portage carers and workers, for training in Portage and for information on the 'Quality Play' training.

● Pre-school Learning Alliance, National Centre, 69 Kings Cross Road, London WC1X 9LL. Tel: 020-78330991. For information on DPP courses and their special needs certificate. Free catalogue, order form and price list of publications, such as their book *Inclusion*, also available.

● The Sarah Duffen Centre, Belmont Street, Southsea, Hampshire PO5 1NA. Tel: 023-92824261. Workshops and courses on young children with Down's syndrome.

● Many voluntary organisations run training courses; contact them for details.